WALKI

Jane Austen's
LONDON

Louise Allen

SHIRE PUBLICATIONS

Published in Great Britain in 2013 by Shire Publications Ltd,
Midland House, West Way, Botley, Oxford OX2 0PH, United Kingdom.
43-01 21st Street, Suite 220B, Long Island City, NY 11101, USA.

E-mail: shire@shirebooks.co.uk   www.shirebooks.co.uk

Every attempt has been made by the Publishers to secure the appropriate permissions for materials
reproduced in this book. If there has been any oversight we will be happy to rectify the situation and
a written submission should be made to the Publishers.

A CIP catalogue record for this book is available from the British Library.

Shire General no. 5.   ISBN-13: 978 0 74781 295 1

Louise Allen has asserted her right under the Copyright, Designs and Patents Act, 1988, to be
identified as the author of this book.

Designed by Myriam Bell Design, UK and typeset in Calibri and Perpetua.

Printed in China through Worldprint Ltd.

13 14 15 16 17   10 9 8 7 6 5 4 3 2 1

Acknowledgements

Copyright holders are acknowledged as follows: Alamy, page 4, and Stephen RIchards page 9, top left.

All photographs are copyright Allen J. Hilton.

Out-of-copyright sources for original prints from the author's collection are acknowledged as follows:

Ackermann's *Microcosm of London 1808–10*, pages 75, 78, 102; Ackermann's *Repository*, various
dates, pages 6, 7, 12, 19, 21, 22, 24, 33, 35, 40, 43, 45, 46, 51, 54, 58, 61, 65, 71, 72, 77, 79, 84, 85, 91,
94, 100, 103, 104, 108, 109; Henry Alken, published by Jones & Co., 1820–1, pages 13, 14, 84; *The
Beauties of London*, c. 1820, page 73; *La Belle Assemblée*, various dates, pages 16, 31, 50, 90; *Le Bon
Genre*, c .1818, page 33; E. Burney, published by Longman, Hurst, Rees & Orne, 1806, page 25; D. T.
Egerton, 'Bores' series published by Thomas McLean, c. 1820, pages 27, 35; *Gentleman's Magazine*
supplement 1792, page 12; N. Heideloff, Gallery of Fashion 1794, page 46; David Hughson, *London*,
1809, page 100; *Journal des Dames et des Modes* 1813, page 25; Joseph Nightingale *London and
Middlesex* Vol. III, part II, 1815, page 67; original playbill, page 70; original tradesmen's bills, pages 21,
28, 56, 62; Thomas Allen, *Panorama of London*, 1830, pages 70, 76; Richard Phillips, *Cries of London*, c.
1808, page 59; John Tallis, *London Street Views*, 1843, pages 41, 47; Unidentified fashion plate, 1807,
page 38; *Voyages Pittoresque dans les Quatre Partis du Monde*, 1806, page 106; Robert Wilkinson,
English Theatres, c. 1816, pages 42, 86.

CONTENTS

INTRODUCTION

My Father will be so good as to fetch home his prodigal Daughter from Town, I hope, unless he wishes me to walk the Hospitals, Enter at the Temple, or mount Guard at St James.

Letter to Cassandra Austen, 18 September 1796.

Jane Austen, after a portrait by her sister Cassandra, c. 1810.

Jane Austen was born in 1775 and died in 1817. For almost her entire adult life London was the capital of a country at war with France (1792–1815), with only brief intervals of peace. And yet London flourished, the greatest trading city in the world, with a population growing at a startling rate. New districts pushed the boundaries of London ever outwards with their fine streets, fashionable squares and spacious churches. The Port of London brought in goods from all over the world to fill the shops with a variety of wares never before seen on such a scale. Wealth, fuelled by rapid industrial development and agricultural improvements, poured into the capital.

Much of this London remains, to be discovered by the explorer of today, and it can seem very familiar – great public buildings, elegant streets, green parks. And yet the London Jane Austen knew, and incorporated so confidently into her novels, was very different from the London we know now.

Kensington, Knightsbridge, Hampstead and Islington were all separate villages. Green fields and market gardens still resisted the fingers of development that pushed between them.

Vast, lawless slums or 'rookeries' existed cheek by jowl with fashionable districts. The only policing, apart from the handful of Bow Street Runners, was by parish constables and private watchmen.

Prisons of almost medieval squalor were scattered throughout the city. The civic improvements of the later nineteenth century were yet to come – London Bridge was still the crumbling medieval structure of the nursery rhyme, shorn of its shops and houses, Nash's great Regent Street scheme had yet to begin, and the Thames ran unconfined by the Embankment.

Gas lighting was a novelty in a few streets, privies were still cleared by night-soil men, vast herds of animals were driven daily through the streets to reach the markets, and thousands of horses filled the city with the noise of their hooves and mired the streets with piles of dung. The air was thick with coal smoke from a million chimneys.

Jane never lived for more than a few weeks at a time in London, but she passed through it often on her way to visit friends and family and she stayed on many occasions with her banker brother Henry. Her publishers were in London and her vivid letters are full of detail about shopping expeditions and visits to galleries and theatres.

Despite her protests – '…the truth is, that in London it is always a sickly season. Nobody is healthy in London, nobody can be.' (*Emma*) – her excitement in coming to Town shines through. 'Here I am once more in this Scene of Dissipation & vice, and I begin already to find my Morals corrupted,' she jokes to Cassandra in August 1796.

The eight walks in this book explore three Londons: London at the turn of the eighteenth and nineteenth centuries, the London of Jane Austen's personal experience, and the London of her novels. They are organised east to west and will take you from grand aristocratic mansions to squalid prisons, and from the theatres where Jane admired the great actors of her day to the place where she found 'a great many pretty Caps.' Following these routes we tread in the footsteps of sulky Lydia Bennett, heartbroken Marianne Dashwood, and lovers Harriet Smith and Robert Martin.

THE LENGTH OF THE WALKS

The length is given at the beginning of each walk, but not the time taken, as this will vary depending on whether or not you visit any of the museums, theatres and churches along the way. However, those aside, all the walks can be accomplished in about two hours at a leisurely pace.

An author at work? Morning Dress for August 1813 in Ackermann's *Repository*.

JANE AUSTEN'S FAMILY

The family members mentioned in this book are:

Cassandra Austen, née Leigh, Jane's mother.
Cassandra Austen, Jane's elder sister to whom the letters quoted here were written.
Charles Austen, Jane's sixth brother.
Edward Austen Knight, Jane's third brother.
Eliza Hancock, Jane's cousin Elizabeth. Married (1) Jean Capot de Feuillide, (2) Henry Austen.
Fanny Austen Knight, daughter of Edward.

Frank (Francis) Austen, Jane's fifth brother.

George Austen, Jane's father.

Henry Austen, Jane's fourth brother.

Philadelphia Hancock, George Austen's sister, mother of Eliza.

SOURCES QUOTED

Jane Austen: the author's letters are quoted with her spelling and
punctuation, although her numerous dashes have been omitted.

Gronow, R. H.: *The Reminiscences and Recollections of Captain Gronow*.
1888 edition.

Nightingale, Joseph: *London and Middlesex*. Vol. III, part II.
Middlesex. 1815.

The Picture of London for 1807 Being a Correct Guide. 8th edition.

Wakefield, Priscilla: *Perambulations in London*. 1814.

Setting out in a smart
Walking Dress from the
fashion plates for
November 1811 in
Ackermann's *Repository*.

OTHER PLACES TO VISIT
OUTSIDE LONDON

Jane Austen's House Museum, Chawton, Alton,
Hampshire GU34 1SD.
Telephone: 01420 83262. Website:
www.jane-austens-house-museum.org.uk

The Jane Austen Centre and Regency Tearoom,
40 Gay Street, Queen Square, Bath BA1
2NT. Telephone: 01225 443018.
Website: www.janeausten.co.uk

WALK 1:
SLOANE STREET TO KENSINGTON PALACE GARDENS

Starting location: Sloane Street.

Nearest tube station: Sloane Square or Knightsbridge.

Nearest bus stop: Pont Street (19 or 22 bus).

Length: 2.25 miles walking all the way; 1.5 miles taking the bus between Sloane Street and Hyde Park Corner.

Opening hours:

- APSLEY HOUSE: www.english-heritage.org.uk. Opening times vary according to season.

- KENSINGTON PALACE: www.hrp.org.uk/KensingtonPalace. Open daily from 10 a.m. to 5 p.m. Last admission 4 p.m.

A Hans Town bollard, which served to protect pedestrians from traffic on corners.

Jane's brother Henry and his wife Eliza moved to 64 Sloane Street in 1809. Knightsbridge was still a separate village – on 18 April 1811 Jane wrote, 'If the Weather permits, Eliza & I walk into London this morng.'

Sloane Street was part of the Hans Town development, built up from 1771. With its well-paved roads and patrolling night watchmen, it attracted prosperous professionals like Henry who was a banker with offices in Covent Garden.

No. 64 had three stories with an attic floor, but in 1897 another floor was added and the house refaced. Despite appearances, Henry's house is still there, enclosed in this later shell.

During that first stay in April 1811 Jane was correcting proofs of *Sense and Sensibility*. 'No indeed, I am never too busy to think

Above left: No. 64 Sloane Street.

Above: No. 23 Hans Place. Somewhere inside is the ghost of the house Jane knew.

of S&S. I can no more forget it, than a mother can forget her sucking child,' she wrote to Cassandra. But it was not all work – Eliza gave an entertainment mentioned in the *Morning Post* of 25 April, which must have been very gratifying, even if the newspaper spelled her name wrong: 'Mrs H Austin had a musical party at her house in Sloane-street.'

It was held on the first floor in the octagonal rear salon and the front drawing room. Jane told Cassandra that she spent most of the time talking to friends in '…the connecting Passage, which was comparatively cool, & gave us all the advantage of the Music at a pleasant distance, as well as that of the first view of every new comer.' There were glee singers, a harpist and floral decorations.

Between 22 April and 1 May 1813 Jane stayed here to support Henry through Eliza's final illness: she died on 25 April. On 20 May Jane, who was again with her newly widowed brother, wrote that she was very snug with the front drawing room all to herself.

She enjoyed the little luxuries that Henry could afford. 'The Driving about, the Carriage being open, was very pleasant. I liked my solitary elegance very much, & was ready to laugh all the time, at my being where I was — I could not but feel that I had naturally small right to be parading about London in a Barouche.'

After Eliza's death Henry moved away but eventually returned to live in Hans Place, just around the corner.

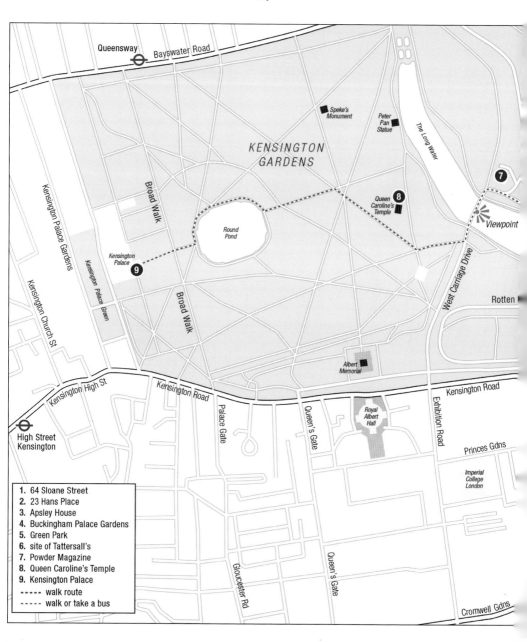

1. 64 Sloane Street
2. 23 Hans Place
3. Apsley House
4. Buckingham Palace Gardens
5. Green Park
6. site of Tattersall's
7. Powder Magazine
8. Queen Caroline's Temple
9. Kensington Palace
----- walk route
----- walk or take a bus

Turn into Hans Street and look at the back of No. 64. There you can see the three external walls of the octagonal room that was the scene of the musical party.

At the end of the street turn left into Hans Place and continue round to No. 23. Jane stayed here for the first time on 22 August 1814.

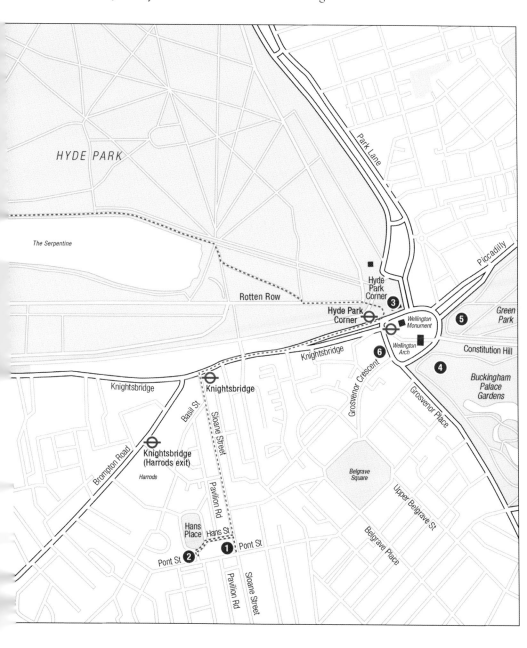

View of Piccadilly from Hyde Park Corner Turnpike in 1810. The first house on the left became Apsley House. Carriages are coming out of Hyde Park beside it; Green Park is on the right.

She arrived in London by stagecoach and was then collected by Henry, in 'the Luxury of a nice large cool dirty Hackney Coach.'

She declared, 'It is a delightful Place – more than answers my expectation… I find more space & comfort in the rooms than I had supposed, & the Garden is quite a Love.' They could even talk across the garden fence to the family of Mr Tilson, Henry's partner at the bank, who lived at No. 26.

Hyde Park Turnpike in 1792 looking towards Piccadilly with Green Park on the right.

'I am in the front Attic, which is the Bedchamber to be preferred.' This was below the present top floor and over the original front door, which was at the side where the Blue Plaque is located.

In 1884 the house was encased within a brick shell and the exterior considerably altered. The plaque refers to 'a house on this site' but, like Sloane Street, the original remains, encased inside its new skin.

Special traffic lights at Hyde Park Corner, both for carriage horses from the Royal Mews at Buckingham Palace and recreational riders.

Henry's study was at the back, with a balcony and steps down into the garden, which has now been lost under Pont Street. Jane did much of her letter writing and proof reading in this room.

It was at Hans Place that the transfer of her business to publisher John Murray was negotiated by Henry during the autumn of 1815. Henry became seriously ill in October and he was moved down from the bedroom floor to a back room where Jane kept him company while she wrote.

Perhaps the illness was caused by the stress of his failing business. The Alton branch of his bank collapsed in late 1815; all the other branches followed it in March 1816 and Henry was declared bankrupt. That year he became a country clergyman and Jane's visits to London ceased.

Tattersall's auction ring: the knowledgeable crowd place their bids.

WALK 1

Dashing amongst the Pinks in Rotten Row, 1821. Ladies ride side saddle; smart army officers and young swells canter amongst the carriages.

Return to Sloane Street where you can either follow Jane's example and 'walk into London' through Knightsbridge (three quarters of a mile) or catch a bus to Hyde Park Corner if you prefer to save your energy for the later walk in the park.

The dominating landmark at Hyde Park Corner is Apsley House, known as Number One London because it was the first house on the Hyde Park turnpike after the toll gate. Built by Robert Adam in the 1770s, it was purchased by the Duke of Wellington for his London residence when he began his political career. When Jane knew this area it was simply the first of a terrace of smart town dwellings that were demolished when the house was redeveloped in its present form.

Apsley House is well worth visiting. The beautifully preserved interior contains Wellington's collection of art works, the lavish gifts presented to him by grateful rulers, and even a nude statue of Napoleon.

Standing outside, look diagonally across to the Lanesborough Hotel. Until 1825 Hyde Park turnpike gates stood just about where Grosvenor Place meets Knightsbridge.

Jane's letter home on 25 April 1811 blames an incident at the gates for giving her sister-in-law Eliza a chest cold. 'The Horses actually gibbed on this side of Hyde Park Gate – a load of fresh gravel made it a formidable Hill to them, & they refused the collar; I believe there was a sore shoulder to irritate. Eliza was frightened, & we got out & were detained in the Eveng air several minutes.'

Tattersall's auction ring was situated just behind the site of the Lanesborough between 1766 and 1865. It became a sort of club where noblemen, gentlemen, grooms and jockeys could be found mingling and conversing, united by their love of sport.

Go through the gate into Hyde Park, which formed the western edge of London during the early nineteenth century. On your left is the sandy track of Rotten Row: take the right-hand footpath alongside it.

During the Season, Society paraded here every afternoon. It was considered essential to see and to be seen in your most fashionable clothes, riding your finest horse or driving the most expensive carriage you could afford.

If Jane wished to view Society on display, this was the place to be, as *The Picture of London* advises:

> We recommend [the stranger] to pause at some spot…from which his eye can command the entire picture of carriages, horsemen,

The Queen's Temple in Kensington Palace Gardens was built as a summerhouse for Queen Caroline in *c.* 1734. Some of the graffiti inside dates to 1821 when the whole of the Gardens was thrown open to the public on a daily basis.

and foot passengers, in the park, all eager to push forward in various directions, and the more composed picture of the company sauntering in the gardens.

In early March 1814, Fanny and Jane drove in Hyde Park and Jane was much entertained, although somewhat put out not to be seen by a single acquaintance.

Before you reach the Serpentine, cut through the gardens to follow the road along the northern bank and over the bridge.

The Westbourne, one of London's 'lost' rivers, flows down from Hampstead and was dammed in 1730 to form the Serpentine. In 1816 Harriet Shelley, wife of the poet, drowned herself here.

On the right, as the road turns to cross the bridge, is a building mentioned in *The Picture of London* as:

Kensington Gardens Walking Dresses from *La Belle Assemblée*, **July 1808.**

… a powder magazine and a guardroom, both of brick, the sight of which if they must be there for the sake of any convenience, ought to be obscured by planting … Hyde Park is used for the field days of the horse and foot guards … and for some martial reviews; which however is not mentioned as an advantage to the beauty of the place, as these exercises destroy the verdure of the park.

One imagines that Lydia Bennett, with her penchant for men in scarlet coats, would have found this a most attractive sight.

Once over the bridge we are in Kensington Gardens, once the private park belonging to the palace. The lake on the right is The Long Water.

Make your way across the Gardens to the Round Pond and beyond it to the Broad Walk, a very popular promenade in front of the palace, as described in *The Picture of London*:

One of the most delightful scenes belonging to this great metropolis, and that which, perhaps, most displays its opulence and splendour, is formed by the company in Hyde Park and Kensington Gardens, in fine weather, chiefly on Sundays in winter and spring … Numbers of people of fashion, mingled with a great multitude of well-dressed persons of various ranks, crowd the walk for many hours together … No servant in livery, nor women with pattens, nor persons carrying bundles, are admitted into the gardens.

In April 1811 Jane wrote, 'I had a pleasant walk in Kensington Gs on Sunday with Henry, Mr Smith & Mr Tilson – everything was fresh & beautiful.'

The unicorn of Scotland on the southern gates of Kensington Palace. The unicorn joined the English lion as a supporter of the royal coat of arms when James VI of Scotland became James I of England in 1603.

Perhaps it was this excursion she had in mind when, in *Sense and Sensibility*, Mrs Jennings and Elinor meet Miss Steele there.

[It was] so beautiful a Sunday as to draw many to Kensington Gardens, though it was only the second week in March. Mrs Jennings and Elinor were of the number; but Marianne, who knew that the Willoughbys were again in town, and had a constant dread of meeting them, chose rather to stay at home, than venture into so public a place.

In Jane's day Kensington Palace was home to various members of the royal family, including Princess Caroline, the estranged wife of the Prince Regent. He stopped their daughter, Princess Charlotte, visiting her here when he discovered she had frequently been left unchaperoned with a gentleman.

There is a collection of lavish court dress and the royal staterooms are open to the public, including the bedchamber where Princess Victoria was told she had become queen – the day the Georgian era ended.

WALK 2:
MARYLEBONE AND BOND STREET

> **Starting Location:** Marble Arch.
>
> **Nearest tube station:** Marble Arch.
>
> **Length:** 2.25 miles.
>
> **Opening hours:**
>
> - WALLACE COLLECTION: www.wallacecollection.org.
>   Open daily (except 24–26 December), from 10 a.m.
>   to 5 p.m.

Marble Arch is close to the site of Tyburn gallows, but by the time Jane Austen was born the procession of the condemned through the streets amidst jeering, cheering crowds was thought distasteful – and, perhaps more influentially, it disturbed the peace of the fashionable residents of the new developments north of Oxford Street. Public executions were moved to Newgate prison in 1783.

Walk up Great Cumberland Place, the location of the American Legation chancery in 1805, and turn left into Upper Berkeley Street. The elegant streets and squares that were developed in the Marylebone district north of Oxford Street in the late eighteenth century attracted gentry, nobility and the higher echelons of the professions. There was a considerable variety in the size of houses available, from grand mansions to modest dwellings like the one where Henry and Eliza Austen lived between 1801 and 1804.

The district also retained some rough edges including a huge cattle yard just off the Edgware Road. The beasts must have been audible, and, when the wind was right, the smell would have wafted over the smart streets.

The Austens lived close to this nuisance in some style at No. 24 on the north side of the street, employing a French cook and keeping a carriage.

Tyburn Turnpike looking eastwards along Oxford Street in 1813. The transformation of Oxford Street into a fashionable shopping street began in the middle of the eighteenth century. No trace of the Georgian era survives except for one pillar at the entrance to Stratford Place.

WALK 2

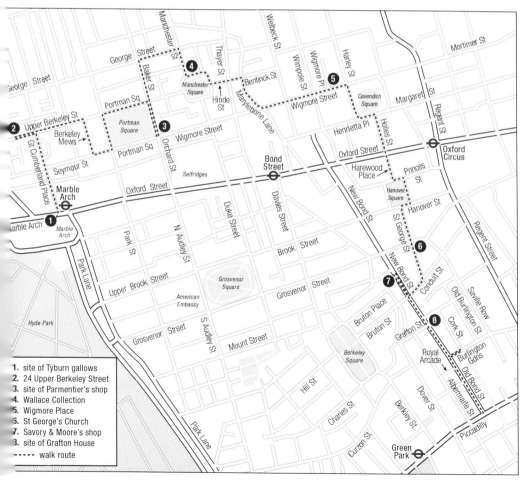

1. site of Tyburn gallows
2. 24 Upper Berkeley Street
3. site of Parmentier's shop
4. Wallace Collection
5. Wigmore Place
6. St George's Church
7. Savory & Moore's shop
8. site of Grafton House
----- walk route

The house is now a small hotel. There is no record that Jane visited No. 24 but Cassandra stayed here during February 1801 and Jane wrote to her, 'I hope you will see everything worthy notice, from the Opera House to Henry's office in Cleveland Court.'

Return to cross Great Cumberland Place and continue along Upper Berkeley Street. Turn right into Berkeley Mews. London was full of mews to provide stabling for the thousands of horses and carriages – perhaps Henry kept his here.

The Mews leads to Seymour Street where we turn left onto Portman Square, begun in 1761. 'The residence of luxurious opulence,' according to Priscilla Wakefield, this was one of the most fashionable addresses in London.

Lord Castlereagh lived here at one time and he was closely associated with Lord Liverpool's repressive government. Shelley wrote of him in *The Mask of Anarchy*:

Henry Austen's house at 24 Upper Berkeley Street. It has lost some of its Georgian detail but the house next door shows how the windows and fanlight would have looked.

I met Murder in the way –
He had a mask like Castlereagh –

Following the Peterloo Massacre in 1819 a furious mob attacked his house and smashed the windows.

Walk around the square clockwise to admire the remaining traces of its splendour until you reach Orchard Street. This is where Jane's aunt, Mrs Hancock, and her cousin Eliza were living in 1788 and she dined with them here in August of that year during her first recorded visit to London.

Wigmore Street leads out of the square at this point, but originally this section was Edwards Street, the location of Parmentier's, confectioner to high Society and royalty. Given her liking for everything fashionable, and with her French taste, Henry Austen's wife Eliza may well have ordered from them when she lived nearby. Here were sold preserves, jellies, jams, fruit pastes, fruits in French brandy, comfits, lozenges, macaroons and rout cakes, as well as ices and creams.

Go back along the eastern side of the square to Baker Street. In *Mansfield Park* this was the London address of the Andersons where Tom Bertram met Miss Anderson, who later embarrassed him with her forward behaviour.

As you walk up Baker Street it is difficult to believe that it was called 'perhaps the handsomest street in London,' in *The Picture of London*.

Turn right into George Street, the location of The Hindoostanee Coffee House, the first Indian restaurant in London, opened by Sake Dean Mahomed in 1810. Despite offering food that was advertised as authentically Indian, and giving gentlemen the opportunity to smoke a hookah, it failed to become popular and closed after a year.

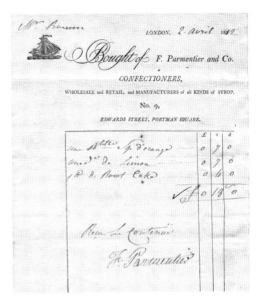

A bill from Parmentier's to a gentleman living in Harley Street, April 1812. A bottle each of orange and lemon 'syrop' and a dozen rout cakes totals eighteen shillings.

Manchester Square in 1813, showing Manchester House, now home to the Wallace Collection.

George Street leads to Manchester Street, the temporary address of the Churchills in *Emma*. In 1814 the prophetess Joanna Southcott died at No. 38. Followers watched her grave in St John's Wood churchyard for years in the hope of her promised resurrection.

Turn right to Manchester Square, the home of the Wallace Collection, a superb gallery of art, furniture, paintings and armour. It was originally Manchester House which was, according to *The Picture of London*, 'one of the best in London'.

Hinde Street leads from the square to ancient Marylebone Lane, winding through Marylebone village. Ahead is Bentinck Street where Jane visited her friends the Cookes in April 1811.

Turn right down Marylebone Lane, left into Wigmore Street and along to cross Wimpole Street. This was the scene of scandal in *Mansfield Park* when Maria Rushworth, who lived here with her dull husband, ran off with Henry Crawford: '… it was with infinite concern the newspaper had to announce to the world, a matrimonial fracas in the family of Mr R. of Wimpole Street.'

Another scandalous marriage began in Wigmore Street in 1791 when Sir William and Lady Hamilton set up their first home together. She, of course, became Nelson's mistress. Ironically, in the same year, Captain and Mrs Horatio Nelson were living just a short distance away in Cavendish Square.

The north side of Cavendish Square in 1813. The chaise with its postilions is drawn up in front of a pair of houses that can still be seen today. This is a typical colour for a post chaise – they were known as 'yellow bounders'.

At the corner of Wigmore Place is No. 10 where Frederica in *Lady Susan* attends boarding school. On the other side of Wigmore Street, No. 11 was the location of Christian and Sons, drapers. In May 1813 Jane mentions visiting the shop to buy dimity, a figured cotton cloth.

Walk on to reach the corner of Harley Street. In *Sense and Sensibility* the John Dashwoods had taken a very good house for the season in Harley Street and Mrs Dennison visits when Elinor and Marianne are calling on them. To Fanny's annoyance she invites the sisters to a musical evening, which obliges Fanny to send her carriage to collect them, a gesture which she feels gives them a most unjustified status.

Harley Street, today synonymous with doctors, had only a few of them in Jane's day. It did, however, appear to attract the military. The Duchess of Wellington lived at No. 11 while her husband was serving in the Peninsula, Admiral Lord Keith lived at No. 89 and Admiral Hood at No. 16. Naval widows Lady Nelson and Lady Rodney also resided here.

The building occupied by Coutts Bank on the corner of Cavendish Square was lived in for many years by Princess Amelia, the unmarried daughter of George II. A little further along on the same side of the square is a pair of handsome Palladian frontages flanking Dean's Mews.

When Henry Mayhew was writing *London Labour and the London Poor* in the mid-nineteenth century he quoted 'Billy' who was, for many years, a crossing sweeper in the area. Billy had seen Queen Caroline, the estranged wife of George IV, pass through the square after her trial. 'They took the horses out of her carriage and pulled her along. She kept a-chucking money out of the carriage, and I went and scrambled for it, and I got five-and-twenty shillin'.'

Leave Cavendish Square by Holles Street, cross Oxford Street and follow Harewood Place to Hanover Square. In *Sense and Sensibility* Mrs Palmer, on hearing that the Dashwood sisters are not coming to Town, protests that she could have found them, 'the nicest house in the world for you, next door to ours, in Hanover Square.'

Statue in Hanover Square of William Pitt the Younger. First appointed at the age of twenty-four, Pitt was the youngest-ever Prime Minister. He died in 1806 having been in office throughout most of the wars with France.

St George's, Hanover
Square. View along
St George Street from
the south in 1812.

One of the plaques
in St George's listing
the churchwardens,
including the Earl
of Jersey in 1794.

St George's, Hanover Square was a fashionable choice for weddings. In *Mansfield Park* Mary Crawford hints at Fanny and Henry getting married here.

The interior looks much as it did at that time, although the box pews were changed in the 1870s. Handel was a regular worshipper and the Earl of Jersey, whose wife was one of the Patronesses of Almack's, was a churchwarden in 1794. Lady Jersey was nicknamed 'Silence' because of her never-ending chatter – perhaps she was quieter during services.

At the bottom of the road is Conduit Street where Sir John and Lady Middleton lived in *Sense and Sensibility*. The Misses Steele stay with them and the Dashwood sisters spend more time there than they would like.

It was also the location of Limmer's Hotel, 'the most dirty hotel in London,' according to Captain Gronow. Despite this, 'in the gloomy comfortless coffee-room might be seen many members of the rich squirearchy, who visited London during the sporting season.'

Turn right to reach New Bond Street. Most early buildings have been swept away but it remains the exclusive shopping street that it was when Jane knew it well. Priscilla Wakefield tells us, 'Bond-street is the grand mart for fashionable items of dress, and is consequently the resort of ladies of the ton, who assemble there in splendid carriages; whilst idle beaux, distinguished by the appellation of Loungers come to gaze at them, and, in their turn to attract attention.'

Two until five was the time for being seen during the Season and Sir Walter Scott, Byron, Brummell and the Prince Regent were frequent 'loungers'.

Jane knew it well and placed her characters here with confidence. In *Sense and Sensibility* Marianne, miserable over Willoughby, is a poor companion on a shopping trip:

In Bond-street especially, where much of their business lay, her eyes were in constant inquiry; and in whatever shop the party were engaged, her mind was equally abstracted… Restless and dissatisfied every where, her sister could never obtain her opinion of any article of purchase…and [she] could with difficulty govern her vexation at the tediousness of Mrs Palmer, whose eye was caught by every thing pretty, expensive, or new; who was wild to buy all, could determine on none, and dawdled away her time in rapture and indecision.

Willoughby is lodging in Bond Street when he writes to Marianne, protesting that he had never intended to court her as his affections were already engaged elsewhere.

The street was full of hotels, lodgings and eating places as well as shops. Steven's and Long's hotels were both favourites of the ton, as members of fashionable Society were known. Byron and Scott patronised Long's dining room and Steven's attracted aristocratic army officers. They were so exclusive that if a stranger wished to dine at Steven's the staff would inform him that there were no tables, whether there were or not.

In the evening, bands of Savoyard Pandeans with their panpipes would gather in the porches and entertain the gentlemen inside and the less exalted crowd outside.

A fashionable young gentleman of 1813 wearing buckskin breeches.

A band of Pandean minstrels showing the panpipes that gave them their name. This troupe is performing at Vauxhall pleasure gardens in 1806.

Turn right, and almost immediately opposite is The Fine Arts Society. Lord Camelford, a noted eccentric, lived over a grocer's shop on this site, and provoked a riot when London was illuminated to celebrate the short-lived peace in 1801. He refused to allow his landlord to light up the windows as the mob demanded and the house was stormed. His lordship threw one man down the stairs before emerging with a cudgel to fend off the attackers.

In 1797 Lord Nelson lived next door on the site of No. 147. He was very ill at the time, following the loss of his right arm at the second battle of Cape St Vincent, and received devoted nursing from Lady Nelson.

The shop front of No. 143 is the original belonging to the chemists Savory and Moore, founded in 1794. Thomas Field Savory was a talented chemist with friends in high places. Wellington and Lady Hamilton were customers and the Duke of Sussex, brother of George IV, often dined here as his guest. In 1815 Savory acquired the patent for the internationally popular laxative Seidlitz powders, which made his fortune.

Turn to walk down to the corner of New Bond Street and Grafton Street. This was the location of Grafton House, home of high-class drapers Wilding and Kent. On 17 April 1811 Jane and Manon, Eliza Austen's maidservant, '... took our walk to Grafton House, & I have a good deal to say on that subject. I am sorry to

**Plaque to Nelson on
147 New Bond Street.**

Savory and Moore's original shop front.

WALK 2

tell you that I am getting very extravagant & spending all my Money; & what is worse for *you*, I have been spending yours too …', she told Cassandra.

Wilding and Kent's was obviously a busy shop. In November 1815 Jane complains of 'the miseries' of shopping there and most of her references to it mention an early start and long waits to be served – not that this stopped her going there frequently.

By the time we reach Burlington Gardens we are in Old Bond Street. Turn into Burlington Gardens to look up Cork Street, on the left. Jane stayed here in August 1796, probably in a hotel with other family members, and wrote jokingly to Cassandra, 'Here I am once more in this scene of Dissipation & vice, & I begin already to find my Morals corrupted.'

Returning to Old Bond Street, Trufitt and Hill had been at No. 23 since 1805 when Francis Trufitt set up as 'court hair and head dresser'. They were wigmakers to George IV and are now located in St James's Street where we pass their shop during Walk 4.

The Clarendon Hotel, Bond Street, close to Wilding and Kent's shop. The officer is accompanied by a smartly trimmed poodle.

Shops with a Royal Warrant were sure to publicise the fact. This account was sent out by 'W. & G. Bicknell. Town Manufacturers of Hosiery, Hats & Gloves to their Majesties, the Prince of Wales, Duke of York and the Royal Family. The Corner of Old Bond Street.' The bill, totalling £7 8s 6d, is for footmen's livery.

Ladies would not visit a hairdresser's shop, expecting the coiffeur to call on them. On 15 September 1813 Jane reported that her hairdresser, 'Mr Hall was very punctual yesterday & curled me out at a great rate. I thought it looked hideous, and longed for a snug cap instead, but my companions silenced me by their admiration. I had only a bit of velvet round my head. I did not catch cold however.'

Gieves the tailors made uniforms for many naval leaders of the Napoleonic wars – Nelson, Hood and Rodney amongst them – while Dollands supplied their telescopes, including the one Nelson used on HMS *Victory*. Their shops were on the site of the Royal Arcade. Another superior tailor, Weston, was close by.

Jane may have enjoyed Hookham's library, opposite Stafford Street, one of the most fashionable of the numerous bookshops and lending libraries in the district.

Almost next door was Gentleman John Jackson's gymnasium where he taught boxing and fencing to the gentlemen of the ton, including the Prince Regent.

Continue down Old Bond Street to reach Piccadilly where our walk ends.

WALK 3:
MAYFAIR

Starting Location: The Ritz Hotel.

Nearest Tube Station: Green Park.

Length: 1.75 miles.

The White Horse Cellar, which stood on the site of the Ritz, was a principal boarding point for stagecoaches to the south and west, a three-storied building with a gallery along the top overlooking the yard. Viewing the departure of the stages was a popular amusement for Londoners and it would have been a noisy and crowded spot.

On the western corner of Arlington Street was the Bath Hotel where Jane stayed in June 1808. She was not impressed. 'At half after seven yesterday morning Henry saw us into our own carriage, and we drove away from the Bath Hotel; which, by the bye, had been found most uncomfortable quarters – very dirty, very noisy, and very ill-provided.'

Cross Piccadilly and look up Dover Street. On the right, just after the Clarendon pub, was No. 6, where from 1810 gunsmith John Manton had his shop. This was a popular meeting place for gentlemen, where they could practise their shooting in the special gallery and prove their skill by 'culping', or hitting a 'wafer' (a paper letter seal) used as a target. His brother, and bitter rival, Joseph, had *his* shop in Davies Street, which enters the north-west corner of Berkeley Square.

The sign over the Ritz arcade fronting Piccadilly.

Brass plaque on John Murray's front door.

Continue along Piccadilly and turn left into Albemarle Street, the home of publisher John Murray, whose premises have been at No. 50 since 1812. He published many of the great names of the era, notably Byron.

Throughout the autumn of 1815 Henry Austen negotiated with Murray on his sister's behalf. On 21 October he wrote from his sickbed:

The Politeness & Perspicuity of your Letter equally claim my earliest Exertion. Your official opinion of the Merits of Emma, is very valuable & satisfactory. Though I venture to differ occasionally from your

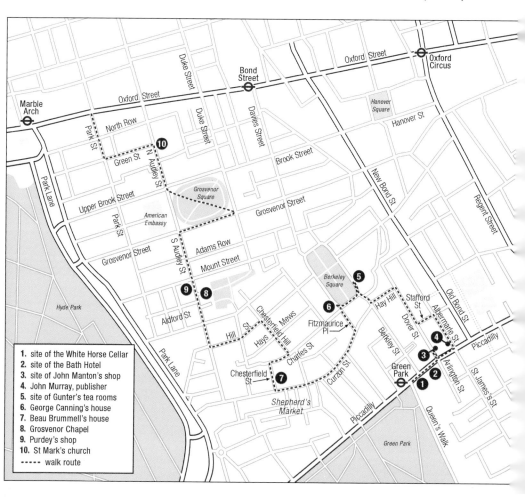

1. site of the White Horse Cellar
2. site of the Bath Hotel
3. site of John Manton's shop
4. John Murray, publisher
5. site of Gunter's tea rooms
6. George Canning's house
7. Beau Brummell's house
8. Grosvenor Chapel
9. Purdey's shop
10. St Mark's church
----- walk route

Critique, yet I assure you the Quantum of your commendation rather exceeds than falls short of the Author's expectation & my own. The Terms you offer are so very inferior to what we had expected, that I am apprehensive of having made some great Error in my Arithmetical Calculation ... but Documents in my possession appear to prove that the Sum offered by you for the Copyright of Sense & Sensibility, Mansfield Park & Emma, is not equal to the Money which my Sister has actually cleared by one very moderate Edition of Mansfield Park ...

The voice of Jane herself comes across very clearly here, even if it is her brother who signs! Eventually they agreed on a second edition of *Mansfield Park* and the publication of *Emma*. Following its dedication to the Prince Regent, Murray brought out an edition of two thousand at twenty-one shillings for the three-volume set. In 1817 he published *Northanger Abbey* and *Persuasion* posthumously, but he remaindered the last copies of Jane's work in 1820.

The relationship was generally friendly – Jane borrowed books from Murray for Henry, including John Scott's *A Visit to Paris in 1814* and *The Field of Waterloo* – but it was definitely a business affair: '... he is a Rogue of course, but a civil one', she told Cassandra.

There were several smart hotels here. Gordon's, on the corner with Piccadilly, was a favourite of Nelson and Byron but the most famous, Grillon's, was opposite John Murray's. Louis XVIII stayed there for two days in 1814 during the premature celebrations of Napoleon's defeat.

The *Edinburgh Annual Register* recorded his departure on 23 April:

This morning, about eight o'clock, his most Christian majesty, the Duchess of

The visit of the Allied Sovereigns in 1814 for the peace celebrations resulted in a flurry of activity amongst the fashionable *modistes*. This is a 'Russian Mantle, Pelisse & Bonnet, Invented & to be had only of Mrs Bell', appearing in *La Belle Assemblée* in November 1814. Vast muffs were highly fashionable at the time.

WALK 3

Berkeley Square and one of its ancient plane trees.

Angouleme, the Prince de Condé, and the Duke de Bourbon, left London to embark at Dover for France. An immense concourse of people had assembled in Albemarle-street at an early hour. The escort of horse-guards took their station opposite Grillon's Hotel soon after six.

Turn left into Stafford Street to Dover Street and turn right, then left down Hay Hill. Originally this was a farm track to the Tyburn Brook. Even after it was developed it was not always safe – the Prince Regent and some friends were held up here and robbed of the not very princely sum of two shillings and sixpence.

At the foot of the hill we reach Berkeley Street where Elinor and Marianne stay with Mrs Jennings in *Sense and Sensibility*. Marianne pines for a visit from Willoughby, but when she finally encounters him at a party he snubs her: 'They departed as soon as the carriage could be found. Scarcely a word was spoken during their return to Berkeley-street. Marianne was in silent agony, too much oppressed even for tears…'.

To the right is Berkeley Square, the location of Gunter's renowned tea shop at No. 7. We encounter the site almost immediately to find that refreshments of a rather different sort can still be enjoyed in a modern building.

Fashionable young ladies choose their ice creams from the menu in a very elegantly furnished confectioner's shop.

Gunter's served exquisite ices and sorbets to eat either in the shop or in one's carriage under the plane trees – the ones that still shade the square are the originals, planted in 1789.

Berkeley Square in 1813. Two servants in livery stand gossiping outside the houses on the west side.

Mr Gunter maintained an extensive garden in Earl's Court, in the village of Kensington, which supplied the shop twice daily in season with soft fruits and exotic – and very expensive – pineapples.

In the eighteenth century the south side of the square was taken up by the gardens of Lansdowne House stretching down to Piccadilly. On the west side is a series of mid-eighteenth century houses with fine ironwork.

George Canning lived at No. 50. He was Foreign Secretary in 1809 when he fell out with Lord Castlereagh over sending troops to the continent. Canning plotted to have Castlereagh replaced as Secretary at War, but his opponent discovered what was going on and challenged him to a duel: 'Under these circumstances, I must require that satisfaction from you to which I feel myself entitled to lay claim.' Canning wounded Castlereagh in the thigh, sparking a political scandal.

Leave the square by Fitzmaurice Place to Curzon Street, which was highly fashionable and still retains some grand Georgian houses. No. 8 was the home of Mary and Agnes Berry, bluestocking sisters. Mary was an author and editor and together they held fashionable intellectual salons, which the Duke of Wellington often attended. As the evening drew on Mary would order their servant, 'No more petticoats', and he would extinguish the porch light, the signal for no more ladies to call.

Just after Half Moon Street there is an entrance to Shepherd Market, a characterful area for a detour. Now it is full of shops and places to eat but originally it was the location of the May Fair that gave this district its name.

A little further on the right hand side of Curzon Street is Crewe House, a rare example of a mid-eighteenth century London mansion that retains its original large site. If you linger to admire it you will get moved along by armed police – it is now the Saudi Arabian Embassy.

Beau Brummell's front door in Chesterfield Street.

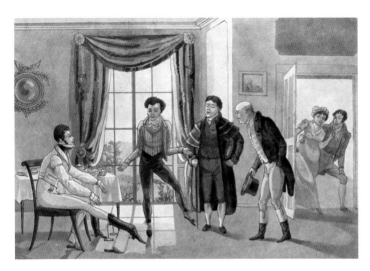

Getting dressed was a complex operation for a fashionable young man. This gentleman has received an unwelcome interruption as he pulls on his tight Hessian boots after breakfast. The parish beadle, accompanied by an aggrieved father, accuses the valet of seducing a serving maid.

A young lady listens attentively to the sermon from her high-sided private box pew. She is wearing Morning Dress in this plate of October 1810 in Ackermann's *Repository*.

The next right turn brings us into Chesterfield Street, an almost intact Georgian street. Beau Brummell lived at No. 4 from 1799 when he arrived in London until debt forced him to move to cheaper accommodation. Even his boot scraper is still in place, and it is easy to imagine him dressing in a leisurely manner whilst chatting to his admiring audience of friends, before leaving around noon for the shops or his club. When it rained, he would have taken a sedan chair – he considered Hackney carriages unfit for a gentleman.

Turn right at the top of the street into Charles Street and then left into Chesterfield Hill. All through this area we are climbing up and down the banks of the Tyburn, which still runs beneath the streets.

Chesterfield Hill retains some of its 1750s houses, for example Nos. 12 and 15. Hay's Mews crosses the street – its size gives a good indication of the number of horses and carriages kept in this prosperous area.

Turn left into Hill Street where Admiral Crawford lived. In *Mansfield Park* Henry Crawford tells Fanny Price that he travelled

WALK 3

Above: Beau Brummell knew this area well. This is a detail from Irena Sedlecka's statue, erected in 2002 at the end of the Piccadilly Arcade, which we visit in Walk 4.

to London to introduce her brother to the admiral in the hope that he would exert his influence to help the young man's career.

Hill Street leads us to South Audley Street, always a mixed street of houses and high-class shops. Turn right to Grosvenor Chapel, one of the eighteenth-century 'chapels of ease' built to serve the upper-class inhabitants of the new developments. Private pews were charged for annually – pew rents – and this gave the speculative builders their profit.

Opposite is Aldford Street, originally Chapel Street. Beau Brummell lived at No. 13 in 1816 and Harriet Westbrooke was residing at No. 23 when Shelley eloped with her in 1811.

Purdey's, the gunsmiths, dates from 1814. James Purdey had made gunstocks for Joseph Manton's as chief stocker and any gentleman who could afford it would buy his guns from Purdey or from one of the Manton brothers.

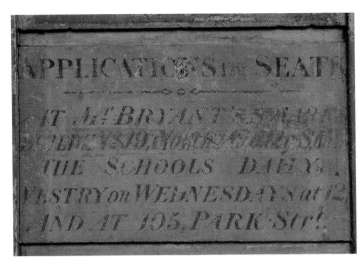

WALK 3

An antique painted sign on St Mark's Church advertising pews to rent. Every respectable family would expect to occupy its own pew with the servants sitting separately at the back of the church or in a gallery.

Opposite, bottom: The present premises of Purdey's were built by James Purdey the Younger in 1880 and the damage to the marble pillars was caused by a bomb in 1941.

South Audley Street ends at Grosvenor Square, the second largest square in London. It dates from 1725, although the houses around it have been extensively rebuilt, and it has always been highly fashionable and exclusive.

Turn right to reach Grosvenor Street. In *Pride and Prejudice* Mr and Mrs Hurst have a house here and Jane Bennett, hoping in vain for a visit from Mr Bingley, calls there on his sister Caroline, only to be fobbed off with the excuse that he was well, but much engaged with Mr Darcy and hardly ever at home.

Cross the square by cutting diagonally across the gardens in the centre to North Audley Street. Follow it to turn into Green Street, opposite St Mark's Church.

Green Street crosses Park Street. On the corner was Park Street Chapel where Doctor James Stanier Clarke, Jane's acquaintance from Carlton House, preached on Christmas Day 1815.

In *Sense and Sensibility* Lucy Steele spitefully tells Elinor that she is betrothed and Elinor protests that she cannot mean the Edward Ferrars that she knows. Lucy retorts, 'Edward Ferrars, the eldest son of Mrs. Ferrars, of Park Street, and brother of your sister-in-law, Mrs. John Dashwood, is the person I mean; you must allow that I am not likely to be deceived as to the name of the man on who all my happiness depends.'

Turn right to reach Oxford Street and the end of this walk.

WALK 4:
LEICESTER SQUARE TO GREEN PARK

Starting location: Leicester Square tube station.

Length: 2 miles.

Opening hours:

- THE ROYAL OPERA ARCADE: www.royaloperaarcade.com. Open Monday to Saturday, 8.30 a.m. to 7.30 p.m. When closed return to Haymarket and walk down to Pall Mall.

- ST JAMES'S PALACE is closed to the public, except for services in the Chapel Royal on Sundays, 8.30 a.m. and 11.30 a.m., October to Good Friday.

- ST JAMES'S SQUARE GARDENS: closed on Sundays.

- ST JAMES'S CHURCH, PICCADILLY: www.st-james-picadilly.org. Open daily from 8 a.m. to 6.30 p.m. but may not be accessible during services and concerts.

- SPENCER HOUSE: www.spencerhouse.co.uk. Open most Sundays, but it is advisable to check.

A delightful display of caps and bonnets from a fashion plate of 1807.

Walk west from the tube station along Cranbourn Street, as far as the entrance to narrow Cranbourn Alley on your left.

In early March 1814 Jane was staying with her brother Henry in nearby Henrietta Street. The weather was miserable and she was thinking about clothes and how to trim her gowns. On the 7 March she wrote to Cassandra, 'Here's a day! The Ground covered with snow! What is to become of us? We were to have walked out early to near Shops, & had the Carriage for the more distant.... Well, we have been out, as far as Coventry St; Edwd escorted us there & back to Newtons, where he left us, & I brought Fanny safely home.'

On that snowy shopping trip she saw, 'A great many pretty Caps in the Windows of Cranbourn Alley! I hope when you come, we shall both be tempted.'

Jane took considerable interest in her caps. On 16 September 1813 she reported, 'My Cap is come home & I like it very much, Fanny has one also; hers is white Sarsenet & Lace, of a different shape from mine; more fit for morning, Carriage wear … *My* Cap has a peak in front.'

A glance down the alley shows that pretty caps are unlikely to be on sale these days.

Continue on to enter Leicester Square. If you turn right and go up Leicester Place a short distance you can compare the view with

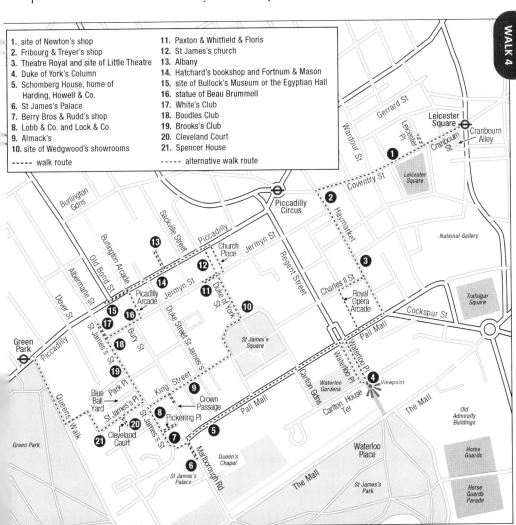

WALK 4

1. site of Newton's shop
2. Fribourg & Treyer's shop
3. Theatre Royal and site of Little Theatre
4. Duke of York's Column
5. Schomberg House, home of Harding, Howell & Co.
6. St James's Palace
7. Berry Bros & Rudd's shop
8. Lobb & Co. and Lock & Co.
9. Almack's
10. site of Wedgwood's showrooms
11. Paxton & Whitfield & Floris
12. St James's church
13. Albany
14. Hatchard's bookshop and Fortnum & Mason
15. site of Bullock's Museum or the Egyptian Hall
16. statue of Beau Brummell
17. White's Club
18. Boodles Club
19. Brooks's Club
20. Cleveland Court
21. Spencer House

----- walk route
----- alternative walk route

the Ackermann print of 1812 before returning to the square. Although Leicester Square today has been completely rebuilt, the focus on popular entertainment would be familiar to a Georgian visitor.

In the eighteenth century the square was lined with aristocratic houses and the homes of leading artists, including Hogarth and Sir Joshua Reynolds. By the time Jane Austen knew it, shops and attractions had arrived including Mr Barker's Panorama, a rotunda 27 metres in diameter on two floors. In 1807 he was showing views of Edinburgh and Gibraltar, in which, according to *Portrait of London*, 'the illusion is so complete, that the spectator may fairly imagine he is present at the display of the real scenery.'

Also in the square was an 'Invisible Girl' trapped in a glass sphere. She could tell the audience, who had paid 2s 6d admission, what they were holding in their hands, answer

Cranbourn Alley today looks very different from when Jane Austen came here window shopping.

their questions and even breathe on them. The Italian soprano Angelica Catalani performed here and more sedate tourists could view Mary Linwood's gallery of needlework 'paintings'.

Leicester Square from Leicester Place. Ackermann's *Repository* January 1812.

Newton's the linen drapers on the corner of Leicester Square and Coventry Street. The window is festooned with shawls, stockings and pieces of fabric.

Continue into Coventry Street, which had good shops that were cheaper than those in Mayfair. Newton's, where Jane and Fanny went that March morning, was an excellent linen drapers and Jane visited regularly. In September 1813 she wrote that Fanny had bought Irish linen at Newton's and she had been thinking of Cassandra's requirements and had found a piece for her at four shillings.

The street ends at Haymarket. This was the main market for hay and straw, serving the Royal Mews and the numerous stables in the area. Throughout the nineteenth century it was notorious for its prostitutes – known as 'Haymarket Ware' – and Miss Austen would certainly not have walked here in the evening!

Almost immediately we come to one of the oldest surviving shop fronts in London. From 1751 it was the tobacconist Fribourg and Treyer and their sign is still on one pane of window glass. The interior retains some original eighteenth-century shelving behind the counter and a pretty Adam-style screen.

Further down is the Theatre Royal. The present building (1820–1) is by Nash,

Fribourg & Treyer's sign survives in the window of their mid-eighteenth-century shop.

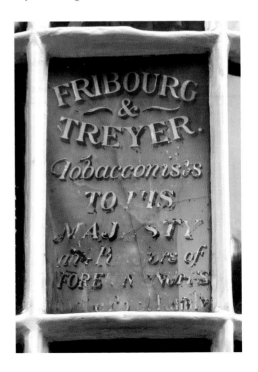

The front of the Little Theatre, Haymarket, in 1815.

WALK 4

The design of the Royal Opera Arcade was strongly influenced by the early nineteenth-century shopping arcades of Paris.

replacing the small one known as The Little Theatre in the Hay. In *Pride and* Prejudice, it is to this that Lydia Bennett refers when she tells Lizzie of her stay with the Gardiners before her wedding and complains, 'my uncle and aunt were horrid unpleasant … I did not once put my foot out of doors, though I was there a fortnight. Not one party, or scheme, or anything. To be sure London was rather thin, but however the Little Theatre was open.'

When the new theatre was built, Charles II Street opposite was opened up to give a clear view from St James's Square. On the left side of Charles II Street is th entrance to the Royal Opera Arcade, the oldest shopping arcade in Britain, built in 1816–18 by Nash and Repton. The interior remains virtually intact and as you walk down it is easy to imagine the shallow bow windows full of bonnets, lace, parasols and trinkets. (When it is closed you can reach Pall Mall by continuing on Haymarket.)

Mounting block on the west side of Waterloo Place. It was erected in 1830 at the request of the Duke of Wellington who was sixty eight that year and perhaps needed some help getting onto his horse.

Halfway along is the back entrance to Her Majesty's Theatre. The building on this site that Jane would have been familiar with – the Opera House – had the first horseshoe-shaped auditorium in Britain and a separate assembly room. *The Picture of London* describes a glittering interior with each tier of boxes decorated differently and the whole crowned with a magnificent dome.

The Arcade ends at Pall Mall. Turn right to Waterloo Place, the southern termination of Nash's great Regent Street project. Acres of houses were demolished and streets vanished during 1816, and with the demolition of Carlton House in 1826 there was scope for even more development. The space gives a good impression of Nash's scheme although all the buildings you see are later replacements. There are views towards Whitehall from the steps by the Duke of York's column.

Carlton House covered the width of Waterloo Place with gardens behind; the screen at the front stretched from the eastern edge of the Institute of Directors' headquarters (the old United Services Club), to the western end of the Athenaeum.

Between 1783 and 1812 Henry Holland worked to create a home of astounding opulence. Even the Regent was forced to admit

The Screen across the Pall Mall frontage of Carlton House in 1809.

the cost was 'enormous'. Priscilla Wakefield gives us a glimpse of the lavish interior:

> The principal apartments are splendidly furnished in the modern style. The grand salon is superb. Four chandeliers, of unrivalled brilliancy, reflect the light to the most remote corner of the room. These lamps resemble a Gothic tower, eight feet in height, without the chains ... The lustre is supported by four very elegant and massy chains, composed of bronze and or moulu. In the interior are four other chains of silver ... the whole taken together, is so radiant and beautiful, that it may be compared to the descriptions in the Arabian Nights.

The Prince Regent was an admirer of Miss Austen's novels and, when he became aware of her presence in London, an invitation was issued by the Reverend James Stanier Clarke, his domestic chaplain and librarian. Jane visited Carlton House on 13 November 1815.

It was made clear that the dedication of her next novel to the Prince Regent would be acceptable, but as a supporter of Princess Caroline, rather than of her estranged husband, Jane was reluctant at first. Two days after the visit she wrote to Doctor Stanier Clarke for clarification of whether she had received a request, an order or a suggestion. 'I shd be equally concerned to appear either presumptuous or Ungrateful.'

Eventually her publisher John Murray and her family persuaded her that this was a royal command and a fine presentation set of *Emma* with a respectful dedication was sent to Carlton House in December.

The Reverend Stanier Clarke became rather tiresomely persistent with suggestions for characters and plots and influenced Jane's humorous *Plan of a Novel, according to Hints from Various Quarters*, written in 1816.

When the Prince Regent became George IV in 1820 he decided that Carlton House and St James's Palace were inadequate for a king and ordered Buckingham House redesigned and extended as his main London residence. Despite the amount that had been spent on it, Carlton House was demolished.

Pall Mall was the home of many superior lodging houses and clubs – Edward Ferrars stays in Pall Mall after his mother cuts him off for refusing to break his engagement to Lucy Steele (*Sense and Sensibility*). In 1807 it was the first London street to be gas-lit in a temporary display for the king's birthday.

The area had a number of galleries and there were frequent exhibitions. The Gallery of the British Institution was established by George III to promote native artists and Jane visited on the same day in 1811 that she went to the Liverpool Museum.

In May 1813 she was amusing herself identifying her characters in portraits in exhibitions she visited. Having searched the Society of Painters in Watercolours exhibition in Spring Gardens for an image of Elizabeth Bennett – Mrs Darcy – she told Cassandra, 'I have no chance of her in the collection of Sir Joshua Reynolds's Paintings which is now shewing in Pall Mall, & which we are also to visit.' She expected, when she did find her, that she would be dressed in yellow.

On 8 March 1814 she went to see a group of Indian jugglers at 87 Pall Mall but did not report what she thought of them.

Pall Mall had a number of upmarket shops. In *Sense and Sensibility* it was outside a stationer's shop here that Colonel Brandon heard two ladies gossiping in their carriage about Willoughby's engagement to Miss Grey.

The fashionable drapers, Harding, Howell and Co., were located in the seventeenth-century red brick Schomberg House, which still stands out in this street of stone and stucco.

WALK 4

The haberdashery department of Harding, Howell & Co. in Schomberg House.

St James's Palace, shown here in 1812, has hardly changed to the present day.

Court dress in 1794. The vast hoops continued to be required even as the silhouette of ladies' dress changed completely and it was only when George IV came to the throne that it was permissible to dispense with them. Ostrich plumes in the hair were worn for court presentations well into the twentieth century.

According to Ackermann's *Repository*, 'It is fitted up with great taste, and divided by glazed partitions into four departments.' These were: furs and fans; 'haberdashery of every description, silks, muslins, lace, gloves etc.'; jewellery and ornamental items including perfumery; and finally millinery and dresses, 'so that there is no article of female attire or decoration, but what may be here procured in the first style of elegance and fashion.'

Pall Mall ends at St James's Palace, the official London residence of the monarch. During the Regency four of the royal dukes had apartments here, although the Prince Regent much preferred the gaudy splendour he created at Carlton House.

Meanwhile the king was elsewhere. In 1810 John Wallis noted, '... since [George III's] last illness, this palace is almost deserted; a levee only is holden here now and then when the king comes from Windsor, for that purpose. Windsor is now the favourite residence.'

St James's was built for Henry VIII and its Tudor appearance is little changed since the sixteenth century. This is where royal Drawing Rooms were held. Eliza de Feuillide, Jane's cousin and, later, sister-in-law, attended one and must have been dressed in all the formality of full court dress with vast hooped skirts – she complained about the weight – and plumes in her hair.

Turn up St James's Street on the right hand side. In Jane's day it was packed with gentlemen's clubs and lodgings and smart shops to attract the modish residents. In *Sense and* Sensibility, Colonel Brandon stayed here when in London.

In 1815, the Reverend Joseph Nightingale described it thus:

Eighteenth-century parish boundary markers on the wall of St James's Palace. To the left is St Martin-in-the-Fields, showing the saint on horseback dividing his cloak to share with a beggar. On the right is the marker for St James's, Westminster.

WALK 4

The west side of this street is chiefly composed of stately houses belonging to the nobility and gentry, one or two extensive hotels, bankers etc. The opposite side consists of elegant shops, which appear to a stranger rather as lounging-places than resorts of trade and the busy pursuits of merchandise …The fact is, that, with one or two exceptions, these hotels are those sinks of vice and dissipation – the bane of human happiness and domestic peace – Gaming Houses!

There were in excess of two-dozen gaming hells in the immediate area at the beginning of the nineteenth century.

There were some more respectable establishments, for example the St James's Coffeehouse opposite the Palace gates, popular with army and navy officers; The Royal Coffeehouse, catering for large dinner parties; the Smyrna Coffeehouse, famous for billiards; the York and Dover coffee houses; Parsloe's subscription rooms with its

The corner of St James's Street and Pall Mall. Berry Bros and Rudd's premises can be seen, marked 'Coffee Mill'. The sign still hangs outside.

Above: Interior at Berry Bros and Rudd; the books recording the statistics of those who came to be weighed on the famous scales, originally designed for sacks of coffee. Now only members of the family are allowed on the balance. A cartoon of the Duke of Wellington inside one of the eponymous boots hangs next to the registers.

Above right: Pickering Place looking out to St James's Street through the passage where Berry Bros and Rudd's old shutters hang.

chess club; and the Thatched House Tavern, where the Society of Dilettanti hung their portraits.

You come almost immediately to the beautiful early nineteenth-century shop front of Berry Bros and Rudd. The perfectly preserved interior has sloping wooden floors and their famous scales. Over the fireplace a Hanoverian coat of royal arms has the misspelt motto 'Dieu et Mon Drit.' Apparently the carver ran out of space when he tried to fit in 'Droit'!

Here the cream of Society, including Byron, the Prince Regent, William Pitt, Nelson and Lady Hamilton, were weighed and records kept in books that are still retained. The original shop on the site in 1698 was a grocer and coffee seller but the business moved into wine in the eighteenth century. When Henry Austen had his bank offices in the area this was the obvious place for him to buy his wines.

Immediately after Berry Bros is the narrow entrance to Pickering Place, an atmospheric little court that was the home of a number of notorious gaming hells.

A few shops up from the Pickering Place entrance is Lock and Co. The hatters were founded in the seventeenth century and have been here since 1765. The shop front dates to *c.* 1810 and there are all sorts of early hats gathering dust on top of the display shelves. In a showcase at the foot of the stairs there is one of the Duke of Wellington's hats and a replica of the hat with a green eyeshade designed to Lord Nelson's specifications after he lost the sight of one eye. The original order book entry and sketch are also displayed.

Almost next door is Lobb's the boot makers, a relative newcomer, established in 1849. Inside you can see the workshop where wooden lasts are still handmade to the customer's measurements. The shop is next to the site of Lord Byron's apartments at No. 8 where he was living when he found himself an overnight success with *Childe Harold*. Lady Caroline Lamb created a scandal when she arrived in boy's clothing to visit him.

Across the road is the barbers Trufitt and Hill, who moved here from Old Bond Street where we encounter them on Walk 2.

Turn right into King Street, the location of Almack's, a cornerstone of Georgian Society. In contrast to this elegant respectability, the warren of courts and passages of St James were home to the courtesans, the demi-reps and the 'fashionable impures' who found this wealthy district so profitable. Look down Crown Passage on the right and you will see a narrow alley very evocative of this seamier side of Georgian life.

Almack's Assembly Rooms opened in 1765 on the site of the modern Almack House, No. 28. By 1800 it provided a venue for men and women of the upper classes to meet, dance and socialise on Wednesday nights – in effect it was *the* 'Marriage Mart' for young ladies of breeding.

WALK 4

An enticing jumble of antique hats on the shelf in Lock and Co.'s shop.

The waltz was considered daring, with its strong rhythms and dancing in hold, and young ladies had to have the permission of one of the Patronesses to dance it at Almack's. This print of 1817 advertises a book by Mr Wilson, a dancing-master, showing how it may be performed, to 'display all the grace, ease, and elegance of which the human figure is capable.'

No alcohol was served, the refreshments were meagre and the Patronesses, who wielded enormous social power by choosing to issue or deny a voucher of admission, enforced the strictest of rules for the weekly balls. Famously, the Duke of Wellington was once turned away for not being correctly attired in knee breeches.

In 1820 Henry Luttrell published *Advice to Julia* with the following lines about Almack's precious vouchers:

> All on that magic list depends;
> Fame, fortune, fashion, lovers, friends:
> 'Tis that which gratifies or vexes
> All ranks, all ages, and both sexes.

Jane's fashionable and socially ambitious cousin, Eliza de Feuillide (later Mrs Henry Austen), attended Almack's. Eliza described herself as, 'the greatest rake imaginable', doubting whether she would be able 'to support London hours, and all the racketing of a London life for a year together.'

King Street ends at St James's Square, part of the development of the area in the 1660s. It was largely rebuilt in the eighteenth century and was highly fashionable. The Prince Regent received the news of the victory at Waterloo on 21 June 1815 while a guest at a party at No. 16. He promptly promoted Major Percy, who had brought the dispatch and some of the French Eagles, to the rank of colonel.

There were also commercial and institutional occupants. Wedgwood moved his china showrooms from Soho to the corner of Duke of York

The showroom of Wedgwood & Byerley, St James's Square in 1809, showing a vast array of wares on display. Ackermann's *Repository* remarks that, 'in walking through the rooms of Mr. Wedgwood, we were surprised that such multifarious articles could be the production of one manufactory.' At this date Wedgwood was employing over five hundred workers, a vast enterprise by the standards of the time.

WALK 4

Street in 1797. In June 1811 Jane wrote from Chawton, 'On Monday I had the pleasure of receiving, unpacking & approving our Wedgwood ware. It all came very safely ...'

On 16 September 1813 she visited in person with her brother Edward and his daughter. 'We then went to Wedgwoods where my Br & Fanny chose a Dinner Set. I believe the pattern is a small Lozenge in purple, between Lines of narrow Gold; & it is to have the Crest.'

Part of this set has survived and, until 2010, was on display at the Jane Austen House in Chawton.

Warren Hastings, the first Governor of India, lived in the square while on trial for corruption. He was eventually acquitted in 1795

The interior of Paxton and Whitfield's cheese shop.

WALK 4

after a seven-year investigation. Hastings was the godfather, and may have been the true father, of Jane's cousin Eliza, and the Austen family were supporters of his cause.

Leave the square by Duke of York Street to reach Jermyn Street. By the early nineteenth century it was full of private hotels and superior lodging houses. When Jane's brother Edward visited London he would often stay here.

To the left at No. 97 are Paxton and Whitfield, cheesemongers, dating back to 1742. Floris London at No. 89 was established in 1730. They received their first Royal Warrant in 1820 as 'Smooth Pointed Comb Maker' to King George IV, and still produce many historic fragrances.

Cross the street to enter St James's Church. (If the church is closed take Church Place, at the east end, which leads to Piccadilly). St James's has links to several significant Georgian figures who are buried or memorialised here, including

A chubby cherubim on the south wall of St James's Church.

SACRED TO THE MEMORY OF
SIR RICHARD CROFT BART. M.D.
BORN 9TH JANUARY 1762,
DIED 13TH FEBRUARY 1818.
ALSO OF HIS WIDOW
MARGARET CROFT
DAUGHTER OF
THOMAS AND ELIZABETH DENMAN,
BORN 9TH JULY 1771,
DIED 24TH SEPTEMBER 1847.

The memorial tablet for Sir Richard Croft in St James's Church.

Sir Richard Croft, who was the *accoucheur* attending Princess Charlotte when she died giving birth in 1817, the tragedy that ultimately led to Princess Victoria ascending the throne. Croft was so harried by accusations of negligence that he shot himself the following year.

Lieutenant-General Sir Colin Campbell, who served in the Peninsula and at Waterloo, is buried here. The poet William Blake (1757–1827) was baptised in the church, which is also the burial place of Beau Brummell's grandparents William and Jane (who died in the 1770s) and James Gilray the caricaturist (died 1815).

Leave the church by the north entrance and you will find yourself in Piccadilly. Cross and turn left towards Sackville Street.

Gray's, a real jewellers of the time, was at No. 41 Sackville Street. In *Sense and Sensibility* Elinor and Marianne are kept waiting in Gray's while Robert Ferrars gives elaborate instructions for the design of a toothpick case:

At last the affair was decided. The ivory, the gold and the pearls, all received their appointment, and the gentleman having named the last day on which his existence could be continued without the possession of the tooth-pick case, drew on his gloves with leisurely care, and bestowing a glance on the Miss Dashwoods which seemed rather to demand, than express, admiration, walked off with a happy air of real conceit and affected disinterest.

The courtyard of Albany where Henry Austen had his bank premises for a time.

Elinor also encounters their half-brother Mr John Dashwood there, only to be insulted by his feeble excuse that he had been too busy to call on them.

A little further along Piccadilly is the entrance to Albany, built in 1770 and converted in 1804, 'into chambers for the casual residence of the nobility and gentry, who had no settled town residence' (*Picture of London*). Byron lived here at one time and Henry Austen had his banking premises at 1, Courtyard, 1804–7.

Albany is next to Burlington House, now the home of the Royal Academy of Arts. In 1815 the house was bought by Lord George Cavendish who was responsible for the development of the Burlington Arcade, which opened in 1819.

Cross Piccadilly to Hatchard's bookshop, established in 1797. It is the only remaining bookshop out of three mentioned in Piccadilly in 1807. 'English booksellers' shops, which are frequented as lounging shops, and which are provided with all new publications, newspapers etc, are Ridgeway's, Stockdale's and Hatchard's' (*Picture of London*).

Almost next door is Fortnum and Mason, started in the 1770s by a royal footman and his landlord. The Duke of Wellington, and many of his officers, equipped themselves with provisions from Fortnum's before going on campaign.

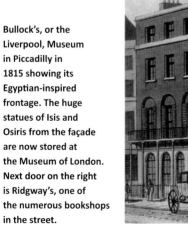

Bullock's, or the Liverpool, Museum in Piccadilly in 1815 showing its Egyptian-inspired frontage. The huge statues of Isis and Osiris from the façade are now stored at the Museum of London. Next door on the right is Ridgway's, one of the numerous bookshops in the street.

Pass Duke Street and Piccadilly Arcade to reach No. 173, the site of the Liverpool Museum, otherwise known, from 1812, as Bullock's or The Egyptian Hall. In 1815 it was exhibiting Napoleon's fabulously equipped carriage, captured after Waterloo. One contemporary guidebook said, 'It is impossible to refer to this acquisition without feeling a patriotic exultation.' The rest of the exhibition seems rather less thrilling – 'amphibious animals in great variety, several mummies and non-descript animals, bones etc.'

In April 1811 Jane told Cassandra that she visited the Liverpool Museum and a gallery. At that time the museum was at its original location at No. 22 Piccadilly. She reports, '…I had some amusement at each, tho' my preference for Men & Women, always inclines me to attend more to the company than the sight,' which rather suggests she managed to ignore most of the bones.

Return to go down Piccadilly Arcade to Jermyn Street and the statue of Beau Brummell wearing his beautifully tasselled Hessian boots and elegant neckcloth. Turn right to the corner of Bury Street where William Brummell kept a lodging house. Through the influence of one of his lodgers, later to become Lord Liverpool, William's son Billy, father of George 'Beau' Brummell, began his rise through society.

Continue on and you will meet St James's Street again. To your right is White's, at Nos. 37–8. Originating in a chocolate house of 1693, it moved to this site in 1755. The building was substantially reconstructed in 1778. White's was the oldest, smartest and most exclusive of the Regency clubs and home to the 'Beau' Window set who would loftily watch the world go by as they sat in the famous bow window. In 1814, during the peace celebrations, the club threw a great ball that cost £10,000. Guests included King George III, the Prince Regent, the Emperor of Russia – and Henry Austen. 'Henry at Whites! Oh! What a Henry.' Jane could hardly contain herself.

A bow window at White's Club. It dates to 1811 and may be the famous window where the 'beaux' would sit to survey the street.

WALK 4

The billhead of an account from Hoby's to Major Crowder, who served with distinction in the Peninsula. A guide to measuring yourself for boots is included at the top right, which must have been handy for customers living in the country and for officers serving abroad. A pair of boots cost Major Crowder £3 16s 6d.

Nearby, on the corner with Piccadilly, stood a shop that seems to epitomise the masculine world of St James's: the boot and shoemaker George Hoby. It was Hoby, who, redesigning the fashionable Hessian boots to the Duke's specification, produced the famous Wellington boot – an elegant yet practical leather creation far removed from today's 'wellies'.

The men did not have the street to themselves, however. In 1807 Mrs Clark, whose shop was at No. 56, advertised '…a large assortment of corsets of every size, and superior make, so that ladies may immediately suit themselves without the inconvenience of being measured.' Fashions in corsets changed regularly and Jane passed on the latest London intelligence on the subject in September 1813. 'I learnt from Mrs Tickar's young Lady, to my high amusement, that the stays now are not made to force the Bosom up at all; *that* was a very unbecoming, unnatural fashion.'

As you walk down the hill you come to chemists Henry and Daniel Rotely Harris, selling some delightfully old-fashioned colognes and flower waters. They came to the street in 1790.

Detail of a window at Boodle's Club. The curved white surround conceals the external blinds.

Next door is Boodles club, No. 28. It was a favourite of country squires and moved here in 1783 to premises originally occupied by the Savoir Vivre, a notorious 'hell'.

Cross the road, taking advantage of one of the traffic islands that were originally introduced in the early nineteenth century to make life safer for the slightly inebriated clubmen as they negotiated the busy, very wide, street.

Cleveland Court off St James's Place, location of Henry Austen's bank premises before he moved to Albany.

WALK 4

On the corner of Park Place is Brooks's, one of Byron's clubs. A stronghold of the Whigs, it moved here in 1778 and was notorious for high-stakes gambling.

On the other corner of Park Place is Justerini and Brooks, wine merchants (established in 1749), and next door at No. 63 was Fenton's Hotel, famous for its medicinal baths.

Further down, opposite the entrance to Blue Ball Yard, is Robert Lewis, the tobacconist, established in 1787. No. 64 was the site of the Cocoa Tree coffee house, later another of Byron's haunts.

Turn right into St James's Place. Halfway along on the left is Cleveland Court where Henry Austen's bank was located from 1801 until he moved the offices to Albany in 1804.

Many of the dwellings in the Place date from the late seventeenth and early eighteenth century but Spencer House at the end is considered one of the most beautiful Georgian buildings in the capital. It was built in 1766 and partly remodelled in the 1780s by Henry Holland, the architect of Carlton House. The elegant interior is well worth visiting.

With your back to Spencer House, walk straight ahead and turn into a very narrow passage just after No. 23. This leads through into Green Park. As John Wallis, author of a Regency guidebook, puts it:

'The Bason in the Green Park' in 1810. The magnificent frontage of Spencer House is on the far left with Queen's Walk running down the eastern edge of the park. The towers of Westminster Abbey can be seen in the distance.

... a favourite promenade ... in fine weather, on every evening and on Sundays in particular, [it] is always extremely crowded with genteel and well dressed company ... The guards parade every day between ten and eleven o'clock, and a full band of music renders this spectacle cheerful and attractive.

Many features have changed since Jane Austen's day, but Queen's Walk, laid out in 1730, remains on the eastern edge. The western part was largely treeless in the early nineteenth century and there was a pool in the central valley fed by Tyburn Brook. Parallel to Piccadilly was the rectangular pond called the 'Reservoir', or the 'Bason'.

Queen's Walk leads up to Piccadilly where this walk ends. To the left you can see the western corner of Bolton Street where the Pulteney Hotel stood. It was one of the best hotels of the day and may even have had water closets – the Russian Grand Duchess Catherine reported with approval, '*certains arrangements de commodité*.'

Her brother Emperor Alexander I stayed there during the visit of the Allied Sovereigns in June 1814 and he was so popular that vast crowds would gather in Piccadilly to cheer him. Cassandra was in London at the time and Jane wrote to her to, 'Take care of yourself, & do not be trampled to death in running after the Emperor.'

WALK 5:
SOHO TO THE BRITISH MUSEUM

Starting location and nearest tube station: Oxford Circus.

Length: 2.5 miles.

Opening hours:

- ST ANNE'S CHURCHYARD: summer 10 a.m. to 6 p.m.; winter 10 a.m. to 4 p.m.
- BRITISH MUSEUM: www.britishmuseum.org. Open daily from 10 a.m. to 5.30 p.m.; Fridays until 8.30 p.m.

A gingerbread seller. The text with this print of 1804 tells us: 'Hot Spiced Gingerbread, sold in oblong flat cakes of one halfpenny each, very well made, well baked, and kept extremely hot, is a very pleasing regale to the pedestrians of London in cold and gloomy evenings.'

From Oxford Circus tube station walk east along Oxford Street to Marks and Spencer's store. This is the site of the Pantheon, which was frequently rebuilt from 1772 and used for masquerades, assemblies and concerts, including the infamous Cyprians' Balls, organised by the high-class courtesans. In 1833 it became the Pantheon Bazaar, finally demolished in 1937. Henry Austen rented a box here, although it is not mentioned in any of Jane's letters.

Continue along Oxford Street, according to Ackermann's *Repository*, 'allowed to be one of the finest streets in Europe; the effect of which, when lighted in the evening, is very magnificent.' Then turn right into Poland Street to enter the Soho district. The long streets of this area fossilise the pattern of fields from before its development in the seventeenth century.

The numerous pubs, shops and the small dwellings, many of them divided into lodging houses, presented a very different London from the smart 'modern' style of Sloane Street and Hans Place, or the elegance of Mayfair. This is a side of Jane Austen's London that we do not visit often in her books or letters, but it was a real and vibrant part of it nonetheless.

When you reach the Coach and Horses pub, pause to look diagonally across to the corner of Noel Street and the house with a mural on the gable end. This is No. 15 where the poet Shelley stayed in 1811 when he was sent down from Oxford. Passionate about Polish freedom, he apparently chose his lodgings by the street name.

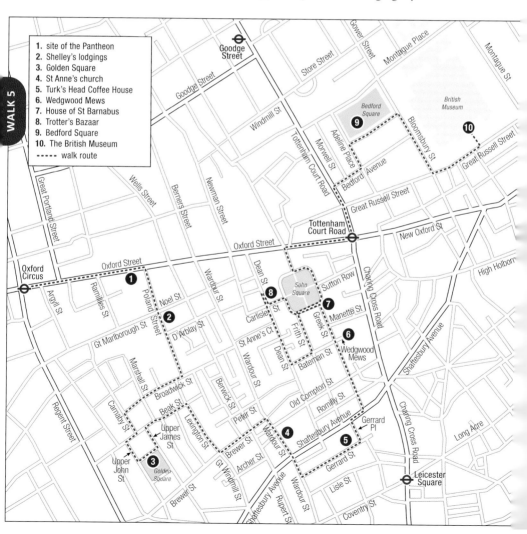

WALK 5

1. site of the Pantheon
2. Shelley's lodgings
3. Golden Square
4. St Anne's church
5. Turk's Head Coffee House
6. Wedgwood Mews
7. House of St Barnabus
8. Trotter's Bazaar
9. Bedford Square
10. The British Museum
----- walk route

Singer Elizabeth Billington, known as the *Poland Street Mantrap*, mistress of both the Duke of Rutland and George, Prince of Wales, lived at No. 54 until 1792. Possibly she visited No. 56, the shop of J. Delcroix, to buy his 'Cream de Sultanes', advertised as 'a preparation which, for embellishing the skin and heightening the charms of personal beauty, is unrivalled.'

Turn right into Broadwick Street and follow it to Carnaby Street, a busy general market until 1820. The area housed Huguenot refugees in the seventeenth century and remained very much a quarter of shopkeepers and tradesmen with a reputation for first-rate poulterers, porkmen and fishmongers.

Turn left into Carnaby Street, then right into Beak Street and take Upper John Street to Golden Square. The house of Doctor James Stanier Clarke, the Royal Librarian who showed Jane around Carlton House, was on the north side at No. 37. In December 1815 he wrote to her to offer the use of his personal library and to assure her that there was always a maid in attendance. There is no record of Jane's response to the shocking invitation to visit an unmarried man's home.

The Pantheon, Oxford Street, in 1814. All the premises beside it are shops: even at this date Oxford Street was predominantly retail and one of the major shopping destinations in London.

An 1818 bill from the Lion Brewhouse in Broad Street, now Broadwick Street. Beer was a much safer drink than water; in 1854 Doctor John Snow finally proved the connection between contaminated water supply and cholera with evidence gathered following the deaths of users of a pump on this site.

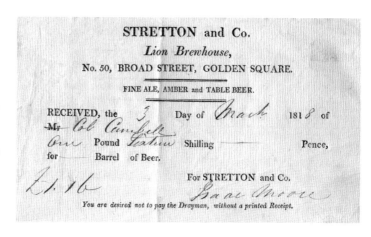

STRETTON and Co.

Lion Brewhouse,

No. 50, BROAD STREET, GOLDEN SQUARE.

FINE ALE, AMBER and TABLE BEER.

RECEIVED, the *3* Day of *March* 181*8* of

Mr *Col Campbell*

One Pound *Fourteen* Shilling ——— Pence,

for ——— Barrel of Beer.

£1.16

For STRETTON and Co.

Isaac Moore

You are desired not to pay the Drayman, without a printed Receipt.

The battered statue of George II in the centre of Golden Square.

Return to Beak Street by Upper James Street, turn right and continue to No. 65, the start of a row of houses with early nineteenth-century shop fronts interrupted by an incongruous pub façade of 1847.

Turning right down Lexington Street brings us to the junction with Brewer Street where Great Windmill Street's curves preserve the line of an ancient track from what is now Piccadilly Circus to a windmill that stood in the fields close by.

If you turn left along Brewer Street then right into Wardour Street you will find the gardens and remains of St Anne's Church behind a forbidding modern screen. From the 1630s to the mid-nineteenth century an estimated 100,000 people were buried in the ¾-acre churchyard: no wonder the ground is so raised. A memorial on the wall remembers the extraordinary 'King of Corsica', a German adventurer who ended his days in debtors' prison, leaving his kingdom to his creditors.

Continue down Wardour Street, crossing Shaftesbury Avenue. In the Georgian period Wardour Street was known for its furniture and antiques shops. Thomas Sheraton, the designer, lived here until 1800.

Turn left into Gerrard Street. Today it is the heart of Chinatown but during the eighteenth century and into the Regency it was full of coffee houses, taverns and lodgings: a focus for creative types. Artists such as John Sell Cotman lived here, as well as actors, including Charles Kemble.

On the left hand side is No. 9. Now a Chinese supermarket, this was originally the famous Turk's Head coffee house, home from home to the likes of Doctor Johnson and Joshua Reynolds. You can climb the eighteenth-century staircase at the back of the shop, just as they did.

Turn left into Gerrard Place, right along Shaftesbury Avenue, then first left into Greek Street to Old Compton Street. This was a vibrant French community during the eighteenth and nineteenth centuries and has always been full of shops and restaurants rather than houses.

Beak Street: one of many early nineteenth-century shop fronts in Soho.

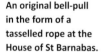

The sign of L'Escargot restaurant in Greek Street, one of the numerous French eating houses that have flourished in the area since the seventeenth century.

An original bell-pull in the form of a tasselled rope at the House of St Barnabas.

Continue along Greek Street, where Casanova lived at No. 47 in 1764. Thomas de Quincey, author of *Confessions of an English Opium-Eater*, ran away from school to seedy lodgings at No. 58 in 1802. No. 20 retains the iron hoist from the original colourman's shop and, close by, Nos. 17 and 21 have early nineteenth-century shop fronts.

Opposite Bateman Street is Wedgwood Mews, originally a late seventeenth-century house. Josiah Wedgwood had his showrooms here between 1774 and 1795 when he moved to St James's Square and opened the shop where the Austens bought their china.

On the corner with Soho Square is the House of St Barnabas, home to Richard Beckford, a vastly rich Jamaica sugar magnate, reminding us just how much wealth in the period was built on the slave trade. Sir Thomas Lawrence, the fashionable painter of spectacular Regency portraits, lived at No. 57 on the opposite corner between 1790 and 1794.

Turn left into Soho Square. The corner in front of you is the one shown in the Ackermann print, although finding cattle and sheep being herded through these days is unlikely! Nos. 33–5, now modern buildings, was the site of the house of the great naturalist Sir Joseph Banks.

Turn into Carlisle Street and right into Dean Street. No. 6 is the back of 4–6 Soho Square, which was Trotter's or The Soho Bazaar and gives a rare glimpse into the warehouse area of a Regency business. This popular covered market with two floors of stalls for millinery and fancy goods was opened in 1816 to help people, especially women, thrown out of work during the post-war slump. Counters could be hired daily at a rate of 3d a foot. It was such a success that it continued until 1885.

Returning along Dean Street, No. 88 is a newsagent with a fine and rare Rococo front – unique in London. Once it must have been a very smart shop indeed, perhaps a music shop, if the instruments in the carving are significant. Further along Dean Street, at the corner with Bateman Street, look up to see the inn sign for the Crown and Two Chairmen pub – a reminder of a popular mode of transport.

Turn left into Bateman Street to reach Frith Street where John Constable lived (1810–11). No. 15 has a fine Gothic shop front (1816).

Return to Soho Square and continue around it to Soho Street, leading to Oxford Street. Walk along to Tottenham Court Road, turn left, then right into Bedford Avenue. Adeline Place will lead you to Bedford Square.

The south-west corner of Soho Square in 1812 with Frith Street to the left. Two men with dogs are herding cows and a flock of sheep with the aid of dogs. Perhaps they are heading for one of the local butchers who served the numerous eating houses in the area.

No. 88 Dean Street retains an unusual eighteenth-century Rococo shop front; it may originally have been a music shop.

Beau Brummell considered that a sedan chair was the only acceptable vehicle for a gentleman to use in town.

Bedford Square is full of very well preserved period features. It was built in 1775–80 and had many distinguished residents.

The Lord Chancellor, Lord Eldon, lived at No. 6 between 1802 and 1819 and seems to have had rather a miserable time. Once when he was unwell he was visited by the Prince Regent, who refused to leave until he had badgered Eldon into appointing one of his cronies to Chancery. Then in 1815 he was besieged in his home by Corn Law rioters for three weeks – they even tied a noose to a lamp-post outside the house. To get to Parliament one of the highest officials in the land was reduced to sneaking through the gardens of the British Museum, escorted by John Townsend, a Bow Street Runner. And finally his daughter eloped from the house with architect George S. Repton, giving the cartoonists a field day at the Lord Chancellor's expense.

Leave the square by Bloomsbury Street, then left into Great Russell Street to the British Museum. The collection was moved here in 1759 to be housed in Montague House. *The Picture of London* instructs:

Persons who wish to see the British Museum should apply at the Assembling Room on any Monday, Wednesday, or Friday, between ten and two when they will be required to inscribe their names and places of abode, in a book kept for that purpose. Five companies, of not more than

15 persons each, may be admitted in the course of the day, at the hours of 10, 11, 12, 1 and 2, when the attendant, whose turn it is, will conduct the companies through the house.

The original British Museum, replaced in 1823 with the building we see today.

Treasures amassed in these early years included Sir William Hamilton's collection of antique vases; the Egyptian antiquities, including the Rosetta Stone, captured from the French in 1801 after the battle of Alexandria (still, in 1807, housed in a large shed near the entrance); and, in 1816, the marbles from the Parthenon collected by Lord Elgin. By 1823 work had begun on the building that houses the museum today.

The Regency and Georgian exhibits are in rooms 46–7 and contain examples of the high style of the period, including jewellery, porcelain, glass and *objets d'art*.

The British Museum has a tearoom and plenty of opportunities to sit down and rest after your walk.

WALK 6:
WESTMINSTER TO CHARING CROSS

Starting location: the middle of Westminster Bridge.

Nearest tube station: Westminster.

Length: 2.5 miles.

Opening hours:

- WESTMINSTER ABBEY: www.westminster-abbey.org. The Abbey is generally open to tourists Monday to Friday and on Saturday mornings, but times vary considerably due to special services. It is always safest to check the website first.

- HOUSEHOLD CAVALRY MUSEUM: www.householdcavalry museum.co.uk. Open most days but hours vary seasonally.

- NATIONAL PORTRAIT GALLERY: www.npg.org.uk. Open daily from 10 a.m. to 6 p.m. Thursday and Friday, open till 9 p.m.

- ST MARTIN IN THE FIELDS: www.smitf.org. The church is open for visitors during the day when services are not being held.

The first Westminster Bridge was completed in 1750 and was considered so handsome that it was painted by Canaletto. The arches gave a good echo and to try it out people would play musical instruments as they were rowed underneath.

One early morning in 1802 Wordsworth was inspired by the view to write the sonnet *Upon Westminster Bridge – Earth has not anything to show so fair* ... You can find the whole poem on a plaque at about the centre. The present bridge was built in 1862.

Astley's Amphitheatre, where circus performances, equestrian exhibitions and popular extravaganzas were held, was located on the far bank. It was rebuilt frequently and finally demolished in 1893.

On 23 August 1796 Jane wrote to Cassandra that she had arrived safely in London and, 'We are to be at Astley's to night, which I am glad of.' Unfortunately there is no record of what they saw or whether it lived up to expectations.

The view downstream from Westminster Bridge.

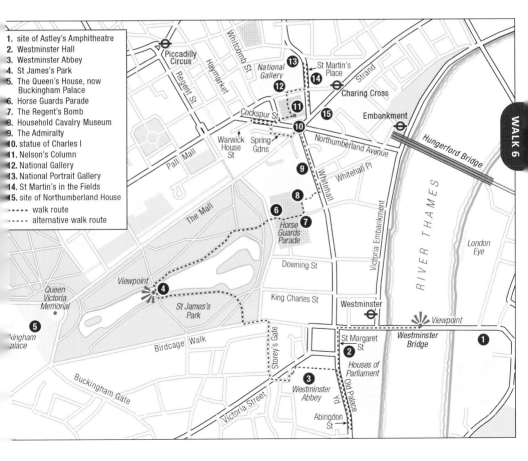

1. site of Astley's Amphitheatre
2. Westminster Hall
3. Westminster Abbey
4. St James's Park
5. The Queen's House, now Buckingham Palace
6. Horse Guards Parade
7. The Regent's Bomb
8. Household Cavalry Museum
9. The Admiralty
10. statue of Charles I
11. Nelson's Column
12. National Gallery
13. National Portrait Gallery
14. St Martin's in the Fields
15. site of Northumberland House
- - - - - walk route
- - - - - alternative walk route

WALK 6

69

In *Emma* Harriet Smith and her admirer Robert Martin are reunited at Astley's. Afterwards his heart was 'very overflowing' and 'she could dwell on it all with the utmost delight.'

To add confusion for Austen scholars there was another Astley's theatre, in the Strand, known by various names including Astley's, Astley's Pavilion and the Olympic Pavilion. So it is possible that Harriet and Robert's tender moment happened there.

Walk back over the bridge and turn left into St Margaret Street. Ahead on your left is Westminster Hall and to the right is Westminster Abbey. Jane would recognise the Abbey but only the great medieval Westminster Hall survived the fire that destroyed the Palace of Westminster in 1834.

A playbill for Astley's Amphitheatre for 10 November 1813. The programme gives a good indication of the melodramatic and exciting flavour of the typical Astley's performance.

In *Persuasion* Sir Walter twice met with William Elliot in the House of Commons lobby and Sir Thomas Bertram of *Mansfield Park* was a Member of Parliament.

Walk down past the front of the Houses of Parliament and when you reach the end, marked by the Victoria Tower, you are in

The old House of Commons seen from the Thames in 1830. As well as a working barge and a small passenger ferry, some pleasure boats with sightseers can be seen. Before flushing lavatories draining to the river became widespread in the 1820s, culminating in the Great Stink of 1858, a boat trip made a pleasant outing.

Abingdon Street. This is where Charles Dundas, MP for Berkshire, lived when in London. Jane knew the Dundas family and it is this, and the proximity of Abingdon Street to Westminster Abbey, that has been put forward to support the identification of a portrait of a lady, with one of the Westminster Abbey towers in the background, as Jane Austen.

Cross the road and walk back towards the Abbey, round the corner to the Great North Door. (If the Abbey is closed, continue round to the Great West door).

One of the most dramatic incidents at Westminster Abbey was the extravagant coronation of George IV. It cost £240,000 and he barred his estranged queen, Caroline, from attending. She became desperate, running from door to door, crying to get in, but eventually she retired, defeated, to Hammersmith.

In *Mansfield Park* Dr Grant is appointed to an ecclesiastical position in the Abbey which – then as now – was packed with monuments and memorials. There are many of particular Georgian interest as we follow the fixed route around the Abbey.

In the North Aisle are George Canning (d. 1827) and Viscount Castlereagh (d. 1822) who duelled over government policy, Lord

State and official horse-drawn carriages still arrive at the Palace of Westminster. Black Rod is the senior official responsible for security.

Westminster Abbey and St Margaret's Church in 1810.

WALK 6

*View of the Bridge &
Pagoda St James's Park
Erected for the Grand
Jubilee in Celebration
of the Peace Under the
Direction of Sir Wm.
Congreave Bart.*

WALK 6

**Buckingham Palace
from the bridge in
St James's Park.**

Palmerston (Secretary at War from 1809 to 1828), and Robert Peel (Home Secretary responsible for the Metropolitan Police force in 1829).

On the left, Abbot Islip's Chapel has memorials to Sir John Franklin (who fought at Trafalgar and led Arctic expeditions in 1819 and 1823); Thomas Telford the engineer; Humphrey Davy the chemist, and the actor John Philip Kemble.

In the South Transept is Poet's Corner. Jane Austen is buried in Winchester Cathedral, but a plaque in her honour is here alongside Robert Southey, Robert Burns, Keats, Shelley, Coleridge, Byron and many other writers.

Following the route brings you into the Cloister and the Museum where there is a wax effigy of Nelson. It was made in 1806 and is dressed in his genuine clothes. Lady Nelson considered it most lifelike.

In the Nave there is a memorial to Pitt the Younger over the Great West Door. Nearby are monuments to Charles James Fox, with a slave at his feet to commemorate his efforts to abolish the trade; Spencer Perceval, the Prime Minister assassinated in 1812; William Wilberforce, another passionate campaigner against slavery; and Sir Stamford Raffles, founder of Singapore.

You leave the Abbey by the Great West Door. Crossing Broad Sanctuary to Storey's Gate leads you to Birdcage Walk and the corner of St James's Park. Enter and walk across to the bridge over the lake.

The park itself was a pleasant promenade by day but at night was a notorious haunt of prostitutes of both sexes. In 1814 it was the site of a series of extravagant celebrations: first for the centenary of Hanoverian rule; then the anniversary of the Battle of the Nile; and finally the peace celebrations following Napoleon's exile to Elba. The architect Nash designed an exotic seven-storey pagoda, which unfortunately caught fire during a firework display, and a bridge, which lasted rather longer.

From the modern bridge there is an excellent view of Buckingham Palace. Jane knew it as the Queen's House and it only took on its present appearance when George IV began its enlargement

The Queen's House before George IV's remodelling to create Buckingham Palace. In this winter's scene there are skaters on the lake in St James's Park.

WALK 6

to fit his concept of a fitting palace. The façade facing down the Mall is twentieth century.

Cross the bridge and turn right to follow the lake shore back towards Whitehall, emerging onto Horse Guards Parade. In 1852 the funeral procession of the Duke of Wellington formed up here, the only location large enough to accommodate it.

To your right the southern boundary is formed by the garden wall of 10 Downing Street. Number 10 has been the official residence of the Prime Minister since 1732 and Beau Brummell was born here in 1778 when his father was private secretary to Lord North. Number 11 has been used by the Chancellor of the Exchequer since 1805.

In the early nineteenth century the Colonial Office was in Downing Street and it was there, in 1805, that Nelson and Wellington had their only encounter. Nelson's thoughts were not recorded, but Wellington was unimpressed by the Admiral's boastful manner.

Between the garden wall and the central archway you will find a squat black mortar captured during the battle of Salamanca in 1812. That battle resulted in the lifting of the siege of Cadiz and the mortar was presented to the Prince Regent, 'as a token of respect and gratitude by the Spanish nation.' The bizarre carriage in the shape of a Chinese dragon was made at Woolwich Arsenal. Regency guidebooks call the mortar 'The Regent's Bomb'. This proved irresistible to caricaturists who changed *bomb* to *bum* and produced numerous very cruel prints on the subject.

On the other side of the archway is a sixteenth-century cannon captured from the French at the Battle of Alexandria (1801). The gun carriage shows a rather strange crocodile and Britannia, who gestures towards the Pyramids.

Next to the arch is the Household Cavalry Museum. In addition to the fascinating collection it is possible to see into the cavalry stables to watch the horses and their riders behind the scenes. Lydia Bennett would undoubtedly have approved of this.

Go through the central arch in the range, which was built between 1750

WALK 6

There has been a collection of exotic waterfowl on the lake in St James's Park ever since the Russian ambassador presented King Charles II with a pair of pelicans in 1664.

and 1759 to combine the barracks with offices for the Secretary at War. Turning left between the mounted guards onto Whitehall, you are almost immediately at the Admiralty, the buildings comprising the houses and offices of the Lords of the Admiralty.

What you can see today would have been a familiar sight to Jane's naval officer brothers, Charles and Frank. Their entire futures, their hopes of advancement, their very lives, were decided inside these buildings. Both entered the navy as boys and reached high rank – Frank as an admiral, Charles as a rear admiral – and both saw service across the globe.

If you look up you will see radio masts on the roof. In the early nineteenth century a telegraph in the same location sent messages down a relay of stations to the fleets at Portsmouth and Deal – a remarkable continuity of function, if not of technology. Regency visitors could see inside the rooftop telegraph huts if they tipped the porters – security seems to have been rather laxer in those days, or perhaps the authorities were confident that French spies could not read the codes.

It was to this building that Lieutenant Lapenotière, captain of HMS *Pickle*, brought the news of Trafalgar and the death of Nelson (21 October 1805). There are information plaques at the southern end of the Screen.

Frank Austen, to his lasting chagrin, was on escort duty to Malta and missed Trafalgar. He wrote, 'To lose all share in the glory of a day

Mounting Guard in 1809, drawn by Rowlandson, who was responsible for the figures, and Pugin, who drew the architecture surrounding Horse Guards Parade.

WALK 6

A trooper on guard at the gates onto Whitehall patiently ignores the tourists.

which surpasses all which ever went before, is what I cannot think of with any degree of patience.'

In *Mansfield Park* Admiral Crawford uses his influence at the Admiralty to secure William Price a post as Second Lieutenant of H.M. Sloop *Thrush*.

Continue up Whitehall to the Charles I statue and turn sharp left into Pall Mall. Ahead is Admiralty Arch (1908–11). Turn into Spring Gardens, the remnant of a pleasure garden dating from Elizabethan days, which originally covered a considerable area at this end of St James's Park.

The Picture of London (1807) recommends Wigley's Royal Promenade rooms here. They were open from 10 a.m. to 10 p.m.; admission was one shilling. The visitor could 'meet' two invisible girls who spoke or sang on demand, or listen to a performance on the panharmonium, a mechanical orchestra.

Rather more intellectual were the exhibitions of The Society of Painters In Water Colours. On 24 May 1813 Jane wrote of a visit with her brother Henry and reported that she was well-pleased with what she saw, especially with:

> … a small portrait of Mrs Bingley … exactly herself, size, shaped face, features & sweetness; there never was a greater likeness.

The Admiralty in 1830. The black masts above the roof in the centre are telegraph towers.

She is dressed in a white gown, with green ornaments, which convinces me of what I had always supposed, that green was a favourite colour with her.

Jane enjoyed finding her characters in works of art and this, which Deirdre le Faye identifies as the charming *Portrait of a Lady* by J. F.-M. Huet-Villiers, made her think of Lizzie Bennett's sister Jane in *Pride and Prejudice*.

Spring Gardens turns sharp right and then enters Cockspur Street. Farrance's confectioner's shop was situated on this corner. It served pastries and ices and was very popular with ladies.

Turn left into Cockspur Street. Priscilla Wakefield tells us that the shops here were, 'of unparalleled elegance, particularly those of cut-glass and jewellery.' A short distance along is Warwick House Street,

Warwick House, 'The residence of a princess to whose hand the sceptre of the British empire will in all probability be at some future period transmitted', according to the text accompanying the print in Ackermann's *Repository* in 1812. The unfortunate Princess Charlotte died in childbirth in 1817.

the drab remains of Warwick Street, which once terminated at the gates of Warwick House.

The Prince Regent insisted that Princess Charlotte lived here in order to separate her from the influence of his estranged wife Princess Caroline. On 16 July 1814 Charlotte, who was in disgrace with her father for flirting, left the house, scrambled into the first hackney carriage she saw in Cockspur Street and ran away to her mother who was living in Connaught Place.

Retrace your steps towards Trafalgar Square and cross to look at the bronze plaques around Nelson's Column. They were cast from captured French cannon and show the battles of Cape St Vincent, Nile and Copenhagen and Nelson's death at Trafalgar. With two brothers in the Navy, Jane and all the family would have had a keen interest in Nelson and the conduct of the war at sea.

From here you can walk across to the National Gallery, climb the steps and admire the view. The King's Mews, designed by William Kent in 1732, stood on the site of the Gallery and the area in front of

WALK 6

Part of the interior of the King's Mews in 1808. It seems more of a palace for horses than a stables.

The portico of the National Gallery with re-used pillars from Carlton House.

Charles I on his horse stares down Whitehall towards the site of his execution at the Banqueting House, while we look along the Strand with Northumberland House on the right (1811).

WALK 6

you was a mix of buildings grown up over the years like coral on a reef. They served at different times as virtually everything from a Civil War barracks to a menagerie. In the centre of the area was the Golden Cross, a large coaching inn serving routes to the south of England. It was all swept away by John Nash's Charing Cross improvement scheme and Trafalgar Square was paved, if not completed, by 1840.

The National Gallery was begun in 1833. The bases and capitals of columns from the demolished Carlton House were used in the portico – virtually the only surviving physical trace of the building Jane visited in 1815 to discuss the dedication of *Emma* to the Prince Regent.

Turn towards the church of St Martin-in-the-Fields; go down the steps and around the corner into the National Portrait Gallery

Despite his best efforts, the Prince Regent was consistently depicted as a buffoon. Even the gulls and pigeons in Trafalgar Square today show scant regard for his dignity.

on the site of the vast St Martin's Workhouse. The Gallery has a suite of rooms (second floor, 17–20) covering the late eighteenth and early nineteenth centuries. Here you come face to face with many of the leading lights of the period, including Nelson and Queen Caroline, both of whom we have met on this walk. There is also an interactive computer allowing you to search the collection so you can find your favourite Georgian character – including, of course, Jane Austen – and buy a print of their portrait.

From the Gallery, cross over to St Martin-in-the-Fields, the only building in the area that Jane would recognise today.

Walk down with Trafalgar Square on your right until you reach the corner, where we end our walk. Jane was familiar with Charing Cross as the busy intersection of Whitehall, the Strand and Cockspur Street. She would have recognised the equestrian statue of Charles I in the middle of the traffic, but the rest of the scene would have baffled her. When Jane was here, perhaps to go shopping in the Strand, Trafalgar Square had not even been thought of. Standing beside her at the end of our walk, you would have been hemmed in by a chaotic jumble of buildings. St Martin's Lane was a narrow street leading up to the church and to St Martin's Workhouse and on the south side of the Strand was the vast Northumberland House.

WALK 7:
SOMERSET HOUSE TO LINCOLN'S INN FIELDS

Starting location: Waterloo Bridge.

Nearest tube stations: Charing Cross, Embankment or Temple.

Length: 1.75 miles.

Opening hours:

- SOMERSET HOUSE: www.somersethouse.org.uk. Terrace and access through Seamen's Hall to the central court open daily from 8 a.m. to 11 p.m.

- ST PAUL'S CHURCH, Covent Garden: www.actorschurch.org/church.html. Open Monday to Friday from 8.30 a.m. to 5 p.m. Saturday opening times vary. Open on Sunday from 9 a.m. to 1 p.m. (5 p.m. when there is Evensong).

- THEATRE ROYAL Drury Lane: for theatre tours contact the box office.

- HUNTERIAN MUSEUM: www.rcseng.ac.uk/museums. Open Tuesday to Saturday, 10 a.m. to 5 p.m.

- SIR JOHN SOANE'S MUSEUM: www.soane.org. Open Tuesday to Saturday, 10 a.m. to 5 p.m., last admission 4.30 p.m. Closed Bank Holidays. Numbers are often restricted, so it is best to check the website first.

- LINCOLN'S INN: www.lincolnsinn.org.uk. The grounds are open Monday to Friday, 7 a.m. to 7 p.m. Visit inside the buildings only with a guided tour (see website).

Tip: Plan your visit carefully with reference to the opening hours above. Covent Garden is very busy at the weekend.

The view downstream from Waterloo Bridge. The ornate spire of St Bride's Church (far left) and the dome of St Paul's Cathedral (both Walk 8) contrast with the tower blocks of the City.

A pair of mermen on the river frontage of Somerset House.

From the middle of Waterloo Bridge there are fine views upstream to Westminster and down to St Paul's. The original bridge, designed by John Rennie, was opened by the Prince Regent a month before Jane Austen's death on the second anniversary of the Battle of Waterloo (18 June 1817). It was replaced in 1937–42.

Walk back towards the Strand and, just as the bridge ends, turn right onto the River Terrace ramp to Somerset House. This terrace – the river frontage before the Embankment was constructed – was inaccessible to the public in Jane's day, depriving them of 'one of the noblest views in the world,' according to *The Picture of London.*

Enter Somerset House from the Terrace through the Seamen's Hall and into the Fountain Court. During the eighteenth and nineteenth centuries Somerset House housed the Royal Academy, the Royal Society and the Society of Antiquaries and exhibitions and art shows here were a fashionable entertainment. Jane had planned to visit in May 1813, but an urgent errand intervened.

WALK 7

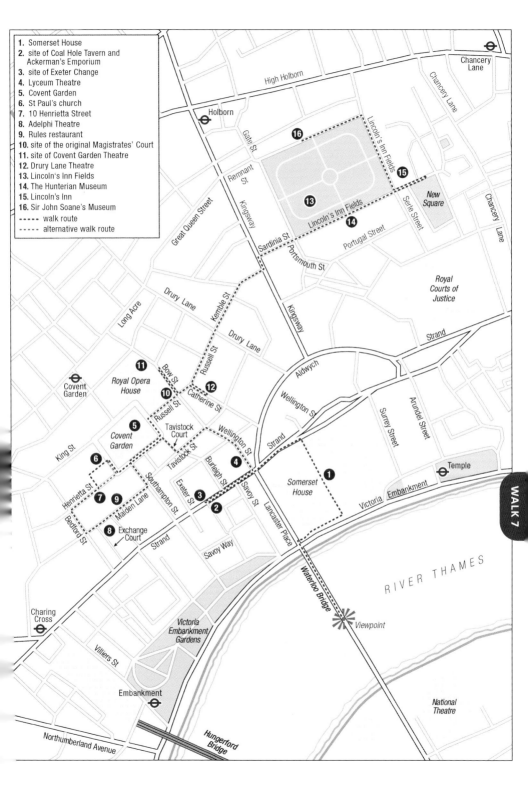

1. Somerset House
2. site of Coal Hole Tavern and Ackerman's Emporium
3. site of Exeter Change
4. Lyceum Theatre
5. Covent Garden
6. St Paul's church
7. 10 Henrietta Street
8. Adelphi Theatre
9. Rules restaurant
10. site of the original Magistrates' Court
11. site of Covent Garden Theatre
12. Drury Lane Theatre
13. Lincoln's Inn Fields
14. The Hunterian Museum
15. Lincoln's Inn
16. Sir John Soane's Museum

----- walk route
----- alternative walk route

WALK 7

A crowded art exhibition in Somerset House with pictures crammed into every space and hung right up to the ceiling in the fashion of the time. This was a major social event during the Season, an excuse to see and be seen.

The Royal Navy occupied one wing throughout the Napoleonic wars, so Jane's brothers Charles and Frank would have known Somerset House well. Cross the courtyard to leave by the Strand entrance.

The Strand is an ancient thoroughfare, dating back to the Normans, but constant redevelopment has left virtually nothing from before the mid-nineteenth century. It was a major shopping street during the late Georgian period, and one Jane would have been familiar with – in daylight, at least, because it had a very disreputable nightlife.

One of her letters records her intention to buy gloves from T. Remnant's shop at No. 126 and she ordered tea from Twining's, whose shop at the eastern end of the Strand we visit in Walk 8.

The view east along the Strand in 1809 to St Mary's in the Strand, with the front of Somerset House on the right.

Turn left and walk along to the entrance to the Savoy. Just beyond, the Savoy Buildings cover the site of the Coal Hole tavern, a popular drinking house for actors and, at one time, a private theatre. Edmund Kean formed the Wolf Club drinking society, which met here. Reputedly it was for husbands whose wives did not permit them to sing in the bath!

Also under the Savoy Buildings is the site of Rudolph Ackermann's Emporium at 101, Strand. Ackermann was a highly successful publisher, coach designer and enterprising retailer. He sold prints and artists' materials and he published the iconic journal, *The Repository of Arts, Literature, Fashions etc* (1809–29). It contains some of the most vivid images of Regency society, including many of the prints in this book. His was the first shop in London to be lit by gas in around 1807.

Cross to the north side of the Strand. Here, between Exeter Street and Burleigh Street, now the Strand Palace Hotel, was the Exeter Change, with small shops whose wares were, 'principally of hardware, cutlery, and inferior jewellery' (Priscilla Wakefield).

Pidcock's (later Polito's) Menagerie, a collection of exotic beasts and birds, was located on the floor above. As the exhibits were mostly live specimens and included a hippopotamus that Byron said resembled Lord Liverpool, as well as lions, tigers, an ostrich and a rhinoceros, the difficulty of keeping them must have been considerable.

In *Sense and Sensibility* one of John Dashwood's feeble excuses for not calling promptly on his half-sisters was that he had to take his young son Harry to see the wild beasts here.

WALK 7

Polito's Royal Menagerie, Exeter Change, in 1812.

The Lyceum Theatre in 1817. There is a demonstration of astrology in progress, typical of the sort of entertainments that the non-licensed theatres put on.

WALK 7

Continuing back along the Strand towards Somerset House brings us to Wellington Street. Turn left here to the Lyceum Theatre. The original theatre close to this site was built in 1771 and, after a spell as a circus, held varied entertainments, including displaying Madame Tussaud's first waxworks exhibition in 1802.

Henry planned to take Jane there on 18 April 1811, but she had a cold and told Cassandra it would be postponed. However, two days later:

We did go to the play after all on Saturday, we went to the Lyceum, & saw the Hypocrite, an old play taken from Moliere's Tartuffe, & were well entertained. Dowton & Matthews were the good actors. Mrs Edwin was the Heroine & her performance is just what it used to be. I have no chance of seeing Mrs Siddons. She did act on Monday, but as Henry was told by the Boxkeeper that he did not think she would, the places, & all thought of it, were given up. I should particularly have liked seeing her in Constance, & could swear at her with little effort for disappointing me.

A shop in this street that the Austens patronised by mail order was Penlington's, a tallow chandlers at the sign of the Crown and Beehive, Charles Street (the name of the street at the time). It evidently produced superior candles, for on 1 November 1800 Jane tells Cassandra, who has just passed through London on her way to Kent, that their mother was 'rather vexed' because Cassandra did not call at Penlington's but that she had sent a written order, 'which does just as well.'

Continue up Wellington Street and turn left into Tavistock Street. This may be where the Austen family went to the dentist when in London. On 24 August 1814 Jane wrote, 'My Brother & Edwd arrived last night … Their business is about Teeth & Wigs, & they are going after breakfast to Scarman's & Tavistock St.'

Tavistock Court leads to the Covent Garden piazza. The Covent Garden area was developed as a smart residential district in the early seventeenth century when the 4th Earl of Bedford commissioned Inigo Jones to create 'houses fitt for the habitacions of *Gentlemen* and men of ability,' around the first open public piazza in England.

After the Great Fire of London (1666), when many small markets were destroyed, it became a major fruit and flower market and the tone changed drastically. The homes of the wealthy were transformed into hotels, gaming houses, coffee houses and bath houses – hummums or bagnios – that were often nothing more than brothels. By the eighteenth century, Covent Garden was a major centre for entertainment and a by-word for vice at night, as well as being a market by day.

Turn left and walk along to the east portico of St Paul's Church. If a member of the Austen family were to stand where you are now, the familiar scene before them would have been one of stalls and sheds – essentially a large-scale street market. The handsome neo-Classical buildings that fill the centre of the piazza were built between 1828 and 1830.

The essayist and poet Leigh Hunt wrote:

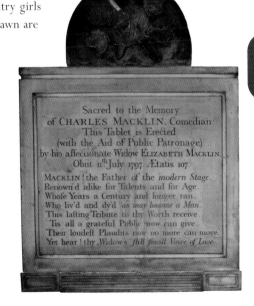

The memorial to Charles Macklin in St Paul's, the 'Actors' Church'. The comic actor died in 1797 aged 107.

[Covent Garden market] has always been the most agreeable in the metropolis … The country girls who bring the things to market at early dawn are a sight themselves worthy of the apples and roses … And the Ladies who come to purchase, crown all. No walk in London on a fine summer's day is more agreeable than the passage through the flowers here at noon when the roses and green leaves are newly watered…

But Ralph Rylance, author of *The Epicure's Almanac* (1815) said that to walk home from the theatre involved 'running the gauntlet thro' streetwalkers and pickpockets.'

If the church is open, enter through the gate into the churchyard. (If the church is not open, turn right into Henrietta Street.)

WALK 7

The house in Henrietta Street where Henry Austen had his bank for several years and in which he lived between 1813 and 1814.

WALK 7

St Paul's, the nearest place of worship for a number of theatres, is known as the Actors' Church. The Austens may have attended services here, for it is on Henry's doorstep, but it is not mentioned in any of Jane's letters.

Turn left as you leave the church and the passage straight ahead will bring you out into Henrietta Street, immediately opposite No. 10 where Henry Austen had his bank offices. In 1813, following the death of his wife, he moved to the apartments above. After the respectable elegance of Sloane Street, living in Covent Garden would have been a startling contrast, although he must have known what to expect. Perhaps the colour and bustle were a welcome distraction from his bereavement. In May Jane described the apartments as being, 'all dirt & confusion, but in a very promising way.' The location does not seem to have given her any sisterly cause for concern.

When she arrived for a visit on 15 September 1813 with her brother Edward, his daughter Fanny and two of Fanny's younger sisters, they had 'a most comfortable dinner of Soup, Fish, Bouillee, Partridges & an apple Tart' – probably in the dining room on the first floor at the front. Henry also had a sitting parlour and a small drawing room as well as the bedchambers. Jane and Fanny shared a bedroom with a little dressing room on the second floor and Edward stayed at a hotel in Maiden Lane.

Jane conjures up a charming family picture on 16 September: 'We are now all four of us young Ladies sitting around the Circular Table in the inner room writing our Letters, while the two Brothers are having a comfortable coze in the room adjoining.'

In November she returned for a two-week stay while Henry negotiated the terms for *Mansfield Park* with Thomas Egerton's publishing firm.

She was here again in March 1814, working on the proofs, and wrote on the 21st, 'Perhaps before the end of April, *Mansfield Park* by the author of S. & S. – P. & P. may be in the World.' It was actually published in May.

The ground floor is a shop now, although the upper part of the façade is more or less as Jane would have known it. The interior was virtually stripped out when it became a nurses' home in the 1950s.

Henry moved back to Knightsbridge in mid-summer 1814. Perhaps, after all, he found Covent Garden noisy and disruptive and the apartment too small.

The royal coat of arms over the stage door of the Adelphi Theatre.

Next door, at No. 9, was Bedford House, the mercers' shop of Layton and Shears. On 24 May 1813 Jane bought fabric there for her mother to have a gown made up – seven yards at six shillings and sixpence the yard. And in September she was shopping there again, looking at very pretty English and Irish poplins, a cloth made of silk and fine worsted.

At the end of Henrietta Street turn left and left again into Maiden Lane which retains a few eighteenth-century houses. On the right is Exchange Court, the site of the artist Turner's birthplace. Further along on the same side is the Adelphi Theatre's stage door. The present building is on the site of the Sans Pareil (1806), which became the Adelphi in 1819. It was popular for burlesques, melodramas, farces

WALK 7

Covent Garden is still full of stalls and crowded with shoppers, but these days they are buying gifts and crafts, not fruit and vegetables.

The view from the boxes to the stalls in the New Theatre (Theatre Royal), Covent Garden.

and pantomimes. Further along, Rules restaurant, which dates to 1798, still serves traditional English food, although in an atmosphere more redolent of the Edwardians than the Georgians.

At the end of the road Southampton Street takes you back to the piazza. Covent Garden is full of shopping opportunities and places to eat and drink. When you are ready to move on, leave by Russell Street on the north-eastern edge. The building on the left-hand corner was the site of the Bedford Coffee House where the Beef-Steak Society moved in 1809. On the right-hand corner was Hummums Hotel, a bagnio with the brothel run by Mrs Gould, a notorious Madam, upstairs. Next to that were Lovejoy's Bagnio and the Bedford Arms Tavern and bagnio.

Turn left into Bow Street, famous for its magistrates' court and the Runners. No original buildings remain: the early magistrates' court was on the western side of the street, where the goods entrance to the Opera House is now. In 1749 the second magistrate, Henry Fielding, founded the band of thief-takers who became known as Bow Street Runners. They remained an independent force even after the Metropolitan Police Act of 1829 and were finally disbanded in 1839.

The Royal Opera House is on the site of Covent Garden Theatre, which dated back to 1732. This burned down in 1808, dispossessing the Beef-Steak Society who would meet there to dine every Saturday evening between November and June. Members included the Prince Regent and his brothers the dukes of York and Sussex. Far more significantly, many of Handel's manuscripts were lost in the fire.

The second theatre opened in 1809. It was so expensive to build that ticket prices were raised, sparking The Old Price Riots, which went on for sixty-one days until the prices were reduced. Mrs Siddons made her farewell performance here in 1812 and the theatre saw the first productions in English of *Don Giovanni*, *The Barber of Seville* and *The Marriage of Figaro*. The present building replaces the one that Jane knew, which burned down in 1855.

The Austen family were enthusiastic about drama; they wrote and performed their own plays and attended the theatre whenever possible. Jane had definite opinions on the productions, and the actors, that she saw.

On 16 September 1813 she told Cassandra:

> Fanny & the two little girls are gone to take Places for tonight at Covent Garden; Clandestine Marriage & Midas. The latter will be a fine show for L. & M. They revelled last night in Don Juan, whom we left in Hell at ½ past 11. We had Scaramouch & a Ghost – and were delighted; I speak of them; my delight was very tranquil, & the rest of us were sober-minded.

One week that month she went to the theatre on two out of three evenings – to The Lyceum and Covent Garden. 'There was no Actor

The Drury Lane Theatre in 1812 with a small group of sightseers on the left admiring the new building.

The door to the Prince's Side in the lobby of Drury Lane Theatre.

worthy naming. I believe the Theatres are thought at a low ebb at present.'

Retrace your steps to Russell Street, and turn left to see the Theatre Royal Drury Lane ahead. Confusingly, it faces Catherine Street, not Drury Lane.

Theatres on this site date back to 1663 and Nell Gwynne made her debut here. The original cellars, with charred remains of the stage floorboards on which she trod, are still intact and may be open if you take a tour.

From 1737 theatres had to be licensed to perform plays and the only two licences granted were for Drury Lane and Covent Garden. All the others had to skirt the law by putting on puppet shows, pantomimes, sketches, burlettas and musical versions of plays. As a result, the pressure on the two licensed theatres meant they became vast, with over three thousand seats each.

A new Drury Lane theatre was opened in 1794 and it was here that in 1800 an attempt was made on the life of George III. It burned down in 1809, the fire watched calmly by the manager Richard Brinsley Sheridan as he sipped a glass of wine by his 'own fireside,' as he wryly put it.

Rebuilt in 1811–12, it is the oldest working theatre in London. Shortly after it was reopened, George III had a furious row with his son, the Prince Regent, in the circular lobby. As a result the management created a separate Prince's Box facing the Royal Box so that each had his own entrance and retiring room. In *Sense and Sensibility* it is in the lobby that Willoughby learns of Marianne's illness from Sir John Middleton.

Edmund Kean's first appearance here was in 1814. On 3 March that year Jane wrote to Cassandra:

Places are secured at Drury Lane for Saturday, but so great is the rage for seeing Keen [sic] that only a 3d & 4th row could be got. As it is in a front box however, I hope we shall do pretty well

Statue of Edmund Kean in the lobby of Drury Lane Theatre.

WALK 7

…There are no good Places to be got in Drury Lane for the next fortnight, but Henry means to secure some for Saturday fortnight when You are reckoned upon.

In her next letter she reports:

We were quite satisfied with Kean. I cannot imagine better acting, but the part was too short, & excepting him & Miss Smith, & she did not quite answer my expectation, the parts were ill filled & the Play heavy. We were too much tired to stay for the whole of Illusion (Nourjahad) which has 3 acts; there is a great deal of finery

The view of Lincoln's Inn Fields from the north-west in 1810.

& dancing in it, but I think little merit … I shall like to see Kean again excessively, & to see him with You too; it appeared to me as if there were no fault in him anywhere; & in his scene with Tubal there was exquisite acting.

The next day they returned and an acquaintance was urging them to go again the day after that. But Jane was coming down with a cold and the performance of Miss Stephens gave her, 'little pleasure either in acting or singing.'

According to *The Picture of London*, boxes cost six shillings; seats in the pit were three shillings and sixpence; the gallery, two shillings; and the upper gallery, one shilling.

Continue along Russell Street into Kemble Street, a nineteenth-century road driven through a tangle of older thoroughfares, to reach Kingsway, which, with Aldwych to the south, was opened in 1905 to reduce the traffic congestion in the area. In the process a maze of ancient streets was swept away.

Cross to Sardinia Street, which leads to Lincoln's Inn Fields, the largest square in London. Halfway along the southern edge you come to the Royal College of Surgeons and the Hunterian Museum. This is fascinating for anyone interested in Georgian surgery and medicine, but, with its dissections and human remains, definitely not if you are the slightest bit squeamish.

Continue to the main entrance of Lincoln's Inn. This 11-acre enclave has been home to The Honourable Society of Lincoln's Inn, one of the four ancient Inns of Court, or associations of barristers, since at least the fifteenth century.

It was to Lincoln's Inn that Tom Lefroy, the young man with whom Jane enjoyed a flirtation – or perhaps something deeper – returned to his legal studies in 1796.

On 10 January that year Jane wrote to Cassandra to tell her about a ball she had attended at Manydown:

> … I am almost afraid to tell you how my Irish friend [Tom Lefroy] and I behaved. Imagine to yourself everything most profligate and shocking in the way of dancing and sitting down together… He is a very gentlemanlike, good-looking, pleasant young man, I assure you.

However, Tom's ambitious family opposed an alliance with the dowerless Miss Austen and Tom was packed off back to London and his studies before things could become too serious. Eventually he became Lord Chief Justice of Ireland.

Sir John Soane's Museum.

WALK 7

Return to Lincoln's Inn Fields and walk round to the northern edge and Sir John Soane's Museum. The architect developed these houses as his own home between 1792 and 1824 and they have undergone extensive restoration and renovation. As well as being a busy and fashionable architect – he designed the Bank of England – Soane was an avid collector of paintings, casts, curiosities and antiquities, which remain in the elegant, and idiosyncratic, rooms he designed for them. The result is a highly atmospheric and evocative Regency experience with which to end your walk.

WALK 8:
TEMPLE BAR TO LONDON BRIDGE

Starting location: Twining's, 216 Strand.

Nearest tube station: Temple.

Length: 2.25 miles.

Opening hours:

- TWINING'S: Open every day except public holidays.
- DOCTOR JOHNSON'S HOUSE: www.drjohnsonshouse.org. Open Monday to Saturday, 11 a.m. to 5 p.m. (5.30 p.m. May to September).
- ST PAUL'S CATHEDRAL: www.stpauls.co.uk. Open for sightseeing, Monday to Saturday from 8.30 a.m. to 4.30 p.m. Last admission 4 p.m. See website for events and services.
- MUSEUM OF LONDON: www.museumoflondon.org.uk. Open daily from 10 a.m. to 6 p.m. Closed 24th to 26th December.
- BANK OF ENGLAND MUSEUM: www.bankofengland.co.uk/education/Pages/museum. Open Monday to Friday from 10 a.m. to 5 p.m. Last admission 4.45 p.m. Closed on public holidays.
- THE MONUMENT: www.themonument.info. Open daily except some public holidays. Check website for details.

Tip: Most City pubs, restaurants and shops are closed on Saturday and Sunday. Generally the area is livelier Monday to Friday.

Historic London is actually two cities – Westminster, the seat of royalty and the abode of the fashionable to the west, and the City, the centre of commerce and finance, to the east. We begin

The entrance to
Twining's tea shop
in the Strand.

this walk outside Twining's the tea merchant, just before the point
where the two meet at Temple Bar.

In 1706 Thomas Twining bought Tom's Coffee Shop in Devereux
Court, the narrow opening just to the west before the half-timbered
pub. Coffee drinking was very popular and Tom's was well placed
to attract City merchants and lawyers from the nearby Middle and
Inner Temples. Tea was less popular because
of high taxes, but Twining persisted in
offering it and began selling dry tea as well
as brewing it on the premises – this may be
the world's first dry tea and coffee shop.

The griffon from the
City of London's coat
of arms rears up on the
Temple Bar memorial,
silhouetted against
the Law Courts.

The original doorway (1787) with its
pair of Chinese gentlemen is a reminder
that all imported tea came from China until
the East India Company introduced large
commercial plantations into India in the
1820s. There is a fascinating collection of
paintings, prints and antique tea caddies
on display and a huge array of teas to try
and to buy.

The Austen family bought their tea
from Twining's. In March 1814 Jane wrote
to Cassandra from Henrietta Street, 'I am

WALK 8

sorry to hear there has been a rise in tea. I do not mean to pay Twining till later in the day, when we may order a fresh supply.' A few days later she adds plaintively, 'I suppose my Mother recollects that she gave me no Money for paying Brecknell & Twining; & *my* funds will not supply enough.'

Opposite are the Royal Courts of Justice, completed in 1882. A few steps east brings us to the Temple Bar memorial in the middle of the road, marking the spot where the Temple Bar gate stood from

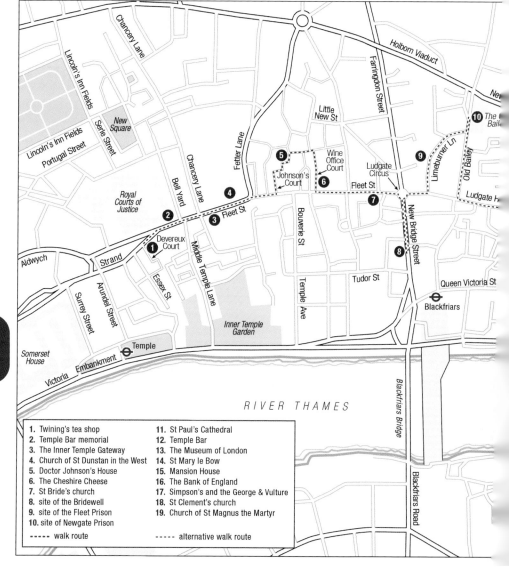

1. Twining's tea shop
2. Temple Bar memorial
3. The Inner Temple Gateway
4. Church of St Dunstan in the West
5. Doctor Johnson's House
6. The Cheshire Cheese
7. St Bride's church
8. site of the Bridewell
9. site of the Fleet Prison
10. site of Newgate Prison

11. St Paul's Cathedral
12. Temple Bar
13. The Museum of London
14. St Mary le Bow
15. Mansion House
16. The Bank of England
17. Simpson's and the George & Vulture
18. St Clement's church
19. Church of St Magnus the Martyr

----- walk route   ----- alternative walk route

WALK 8

1351 until 1878. This is the beginning of the City of London and even today, on ceremonial occasions, the monarch stops here to ask permission to enter the City. In return the Lord Mayor offers his Sword of State as a token of his allegiance. Ornate rests for these swords can be found in most City churches, for example in St Clement's, which we visit later on this walk.

The Bar, which was draped in black velvet for Nelson's funeral, was moved because it had become an obstruction to traffic – we will

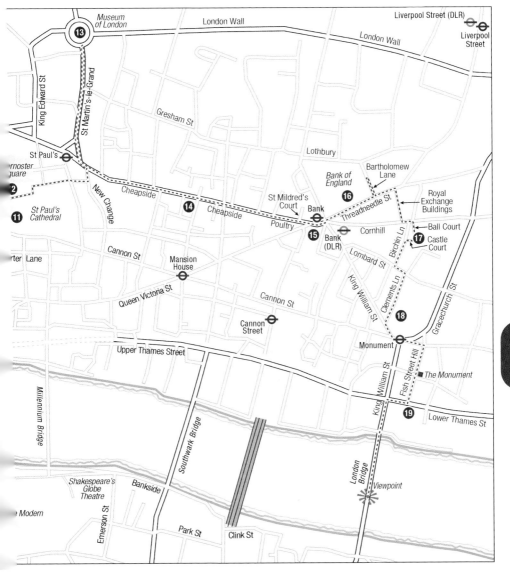

Prince Henry's Room above Inner Temple Gateway in 1807 with the advertisement for Mrs Salmon's Waxworks.

find it during this walk by St Paul's. In *Persuasion* young Mr Elliot had chambers close by and, just past the Bar on the right hand side, there is the pedestrian entrance to Middle Temple Lane leading down to two of the Inns of Court, self-regulating societies of barristers.

The gatehouse should be open Monday to Friday and a diversion into Middle and Inner Temple reveals ancient buildings and some lovely gardens.

Looking west along Fleet Street in 1812. Temple Bar is still in position and the old St Dunstan's Church is squashed in behind shops on the right.

Staying on Fleet Street we come to the Inner Temple Gateway. This is a genuine survivor of the Great Fire and was built in 1610 (restored 1900). It contains Prince Henry's Room, a panelled chamber with the Prince of Wales feathers in the plasterwork ceiling. In Jane Austen's day it was the home of Mrs Salmon's Waxworks.

This collection, created in 1711, moved here in 1795. The displays included the execution of Charles I and a weird assortment of grotesque tableaux, some models even animated by clockwork. They included, 'Margaret Countess of Heningbergh, Lying on a Bed of State, with her three hundred and Sixty-Five Children, all born at one Birth.'

WALK 8

A little further along, John Murray had his office at No. 32 on the corner of Falcon Court from 1762 until the move to Albemarle Street in 1812, a few years before he became Jane's publisher.

When you reach St Dunstan's Church, cross the road to look back the way you have come and compare the view with the print showing Temple Bar as it was in 1812. The old church was rebuilt in 1834 but the 1671 clock remains.

Continuing on the same side of the road we pass small courts and alleys, many of them named after long-vanished inns. Turn into Johnson's Court and continue up to Gough Square and Doctor Johnson's House.

From here you can make your way to Wine Office Court and Ye Olde Cheshire Cheese, a favourite haunt of his. It began life as houses, built just after the Great Fire, but the façade onto the Court is eighteenth century. The interior is highly atmospheric, although the fittings are mostly early to mid-nineteenth century, rather than dating from Johnson's day. It certainly gives an excellent idea of what a tavern interior must have been like in Jane's time.

The elaborate 'wedding cake' tiers of St Bride's spire seen from Ludgate Circus.

Rejoin Fleet Street, which leads us downhill into the valley of the River Fleet at Ludgate Circus. If you look up to the right as you descend you will see the Wren spire of St Bride's Church. The legend is that it inspired Mr Rich, a Georgian pastry cook, to create the tiered wedding cakes that are now traditional.

Pause when you reach Ludgate Circus, built in 1864–75 on the site of the Fleet Bridge. To your left is Farringdon Street, formerly Fleet Market. The river was gradually covered over to give space for stalls until, by 1829, it was reduced to the mere drain that still runs down to the Thames beneath your feet.

WALK 8

The Pass-Room at the Bridewell in 1808. Single women with their babies are locked up for their 'loose behaviour'. At least they had their own beds, even if the mattresses were simply a pile of straw.

To the right is New Bridge Street, constructed in 1764 over the lower part of the river, which by then had become a foetid sewer. The new street provided access to the first Blackfriars Bridge, opened in 1769. It was replaced with the present bridge in 1869.

On the right-hand side as you look down to the bridge was the notorious Alsatia district, a haven for criminals where the authorities feared to tread, and the Bridewell. Built as a royal palace under Henry VIII, after 1556 it became a prison for vagrants, disorderly women and petty criminals until it was closed in 1855. The gatehouse of 1808, improbably elegant for such an institution and the only remains of the Bridewell, is a short way down the hill at No. 14.

Priscilla Wakefield says, 'Many of the prisoners, whom we were permitted to see, were women, young, beautiful and depraved.' These were part of the army of prostitutes who scraped a living in London, many of them girls who had been dismissed from more respectable employment after becoming pregnant.

Jane was well aware of the dangers to innocent young women from procuresses. In September 1796 she wrote to Cassandra joking of the dangers of finding herself alone in London. 'I should inevitably fall a Sacrifice to the arts of some fat Woman who would make me drunk with Small Beer.'

Nor does she flinch from discussing the dangers that awaited young women who 'fell', such as the daughter of Colonel Brandon's sister-in-law, in *Sense and Sensibility*. The Colonel tells Elinor, 'He had left the girl whose youth and innocence he had seduced, in a situation of the utmost distress, with no creditable home, no help, no friends …' Fortunately Brandon rescues her or she could have ended up in a place like this. No wonder the Bennetts were so desperate to find Lydia when she ran away with Wickham in *Pride and Prejudice*.

From Ludgate Circus walk up Ludgate Hill turning into Limeburner Lane, the first street on the left. This follows the south-eastern boundary of the Fleet Prison, and the curve retains the shape of the prison's walls. Conditions in the Fleet, which dated back to the twelfth century, were dreadful, even after it was rebuilt in the 1780s. It was finally closed in 1842.

On the right is the site of Belle Sauvage Yard. The Belle Sauvage was rebuilt by 1676 after the Great Fire and throughout the eighteenth and early nineteenth century was one of the principal coaching inns in the City, with stables for over one hundred horses. Coaches departed for Bath, Cambridge, Cheltenham, Hastings, Leeds and many other

The Old Bailey in 1814. The Sessions House is on the right with Newgate Prison beyond it. Opposite was St Sepulchre's Church, whose bells were tolled as prisoners were led to their execution. Next door to the church was the house of the notorious thief-taker and criminal, Jonathan Wild.

WALK 8

destinations and it became a tourist attraction to watch them leave. The inn was demolished in 1873.

Turn left into the Old Bailey, which brings you to the Central Criminal Courts (1907). This occupies the site of Newgate Prison, another fearsome gaol dating back to the early Middle Ages. A new prison was built (1770–8) and rebuilt (1780–3) after the Gordon Riots, with the Sessions House beside it and an area in front for the vast crowds who gathered for public hangings.

Priscilla Wakefield smugly informs us:

A cell door from Newgate Prison, on display in the Museum of London.

> Humanity pointed out the disadvantage of conveying the wretched sufferers so far from their prison to be put to death; and the use of the gallows [at Tyburn] was laid aside for a new invention, placed on the outside of the prison at Newgate; for in this happy country no capital punishment can be inflicted privately.

The area teemed with spectators during executions, and viewpoints at nearby windows commanded premium prices. In 1807 the crowd was so great that panic set in and twenty-seven people were killed.

For magistrate Henry Fielding, Newgate was, 'a prototype of hell' and the posies of flowers that the judges at the Central Criminal Courts still carry on ceremonial occasions were originally an attempt to ward off the appalling stench of the place.

St Paul's Cathedral in 1814.

The dramatic memorial to Sir William Ponsonby in the crypt of St Paul's Cathedral. He was killed at the battle of Waterloo on 18 June 1815.

Despite the grim surroundings – or perhaps because of the excellent business during court sittings and public hangings – the Old Bailey had numerous eating places, including William's boiled beef shop serving Georgian fast food, the 'hasty dinner'.

Return down Old Bailey to Ludgate Hill and continue to St Paul's Churchyard, the traditional location for booksellers and printers. It was to his uncle Stephen Austen's shop here, 'at the sign of the Angel and Bible', that Jane's newly orphaned father George was sent in 1737, with his two little sisters. They were received 'with neglect, if not with positive unkindness', he later recalled.

The Cathedral has numerous monuments of Georgian interest. Amongst the memorials in the main body of the building are many dating to the war with France, including the admirals Collingwood and Howe. The artist Turner is also buried here. In the Crypt are the massive tombs of Wellington and Nelson.

There is free entrance on the north side to part of the Crypt with loos and a café. Almost opposite this entrance is the re-sited Temple Bar, placed here in 2004.

Leave the cathedral and walk along its northern side to reach New Change. At this point it is possible to make a detour up St Martin le Grand to the Museum of London. The Modern galleries at the museum cover the eighteenth century onwards, and include a door from Newgate and artefacts including a fan celebrating George III's

City street names frequently reflect the trades that were carried on there in the Middle Ages.

WALK 8

	MILK STREET EC2
	FISH STREET HILL EC3
	BREAD STREET EC4
	POULTRY EC2
	IRONMONGER LANE EC2

escape from assassination at Drury Lane Theatre (Walk 7) and one of John Manton's duelling pistols (Walk 3). It is possible to cover the eighteenth century and Regency area in an hour, but allow much longer for the whole museum. There is a café and a shop with a good book section.

To continue on the main route, cross to Cheapside, the street that the Bingley sisters laugh about so snobbishly in *Pride and Prejudice* when they discover that the Bennett girls have an aunt and uncle living in the City.

'If they had uncles enough to fill all Cheapside,' cried Bingley, 'it would not make them one jot less agreeable.'
'But it must very materially lessen their chances of marrying men of any consideration in the world,' replied Darcy.

A London merchant couple in their modest but respectable clothes, portrayed by a French artist in 1804. A ship, the symbol of trade, sails on the Thames behind them.

WALK 8

For all the sneers it was actually a very prosperous and respectable commercial and shopping area.

On the right-hand side is the Wren church of St Mary le Bow. Tradition has it that to be considered a Cockney a Londoner must be born within the sound of its bells.

Lions guarding a heap of coins on one of the Bank's external walls.

Cheapside becomes Poultry, which was the location of the ancient King's Head Tavern. It was famous as the principal turtle depot, with tanks of them in the courtyard, ready to be sent out to make luxurious soup. Elizabeth Fry, the prison reformer, lived at St Mildred's Court at the end of Poultry, almost opposite Mansion House, official residence of the Lord Mayor since 1752.

Cross to Threadneedle Street and the Bank of England looms on your left. Built in 1788 by Sir John Soane, only the great outer wall remains of his design: the interior was rebuilt in the twentieth century.

The George and Vulture.

Turn left into Bartholomew Lane to the entrance to the Bank's museum. There is plenty for the Georgian and Regency enthusiast to enjoy, from coins and banknotes to cartoons.

Continue your walk by crossing Threadneedle Street, through Royal Exchange Buildings to Cornhill. Cross Cornhill and turn left to the narrow entrance of Ball Court.

WALK 8

Modern Fish Street Hill.

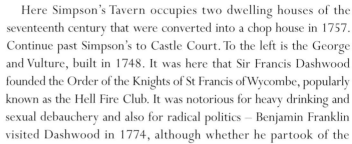

Here Simpson's Tavern occupies two dwelling houses of the seventeenth century that were converted into a chop house in 1757. Continue past Simpson's to Castle Court. To the left is the George and Vulture, built in 1748. It was here that Sir Francis Dashwood founded the Order of the Knights of St Francis of Wycombe, popularly known as the Hell Fire Club. It was notorious for heavy drinking and sexual debauchery and also for radical politics – Benjamin Franklin visited Dashwood in 1774, although whether he partook of the Order's activities is not recorded.

Turn right to Birchin Lane, which leads to Lombard Street; then turn left into Clement's Lane. St Clement's Church is probably the church where Lydia and Wickham were married in *Pride and Prejudice*, although St Clement Danes is also possible. However, this church is just around the corner from where her aunt and uncle lived.

In 1812 Fish Street Hill plunges down past the Monument, under the clock of St Magnus the Martyr and straight onto Old London Bridge.

We were married, you know, at St Clement's, because Wickham's lodgings were in that parish. And it was settled that we should all be there by eleven o'clock. My uncle and aunt and I were to go together; and the others were to meet us at the church.

Then Lydia reveals that Mr Darcy was there also, throwing Lizzie into confusion.

From Clement's Lane bear left to the corner of Gracechurch Street, home of the Bennett girls' Uncle and Aunt Gardiner. 'Mr Darcy may have heard of a place called Gracechurch Street, but he would hardly think a month's ablution enough to cleanse him from its impurities.'

WALK 8

Cross the road and walk down Fish Street Hill past the Monument. This was the bustling thoroughfare that ran down to London Bridge before the old bridge was demolished in 1831–3. At the bottom is Lower Thames Street and the church of St Magnus the Martyr: its large clock, which seems so awkwardly placed now, actually overhung the roadway of Old London Bridge.

Old London Bridge from the Southwark bank. The tower of St Magnus the Martyr and the Monument dominate the skyline.

Turn right and immediately under the modern bridge are steps up to the top. Old London Bridge was just downstream of the present bridge. At the site of the new bridge there was a waterworks with waterwheels taking four million gallons a day from the river to supply ten thousand customers.

Although it was shorn of its famous buildings, and had been widened and refaced in the mid-eighteenth century, the bridge when Jane knew it was still the famous structure of the nursery rhyme.

It was so narrow that traffic jams were common. As a result there were many coaching inns south of the river in Borough High Street where passengers could change to more convenient transport.

The bridge was constantly under repair. It was severely damaged in the winter of 1813–14 when the last frost fair was held on the river; work on its replacement was begun in 1824. The current bridge, where we end our walk, was opened in 1973.

WALK 8

INDEX